REAL COUNTRY

From the Fast Track to Appalachia

REAL

COUNTRY

From the Fast Track to Appalachia

Leslie Brunetsky

Mill City Press, Inc.
212 3rd Avenue North, Suite 570
Minneapolis, MN 55401
612.455.2294
www.millcitypublishing.com

ISBN - 978-1-934937-48-8
ISBN - 1-934937-48-7
LCCN - 2008943113

Cover Illustration by Joe Burleson, burlesongraphics@charter.net
Cover Design by Alan Pranke
Typeset by Peggy LeTrent

Printed in the United States of America

TABLE OF CONTENTS

ACKNOWLEDGEMENTS

My Newark, New Jersey neighbors gave me my first taste of real country by buying more Girl Scout cookies from me than the other Brownies, enabling me to win a scholarship to Camp Kalmia. It was there that I first experienced life without concrete and the start of my love affair with mountains. That romance was further nourished through my high school and college years by the wonderful girls and women I worked with during summers at Camp Navarac in the Saranac Lake area of New York's Adirondack Mountains.

Friends with whom I have shared the experiences of adjusting to life in Appalachia have encouraged me to write this book. Whether folly or wisdom, I am grateful for their support.

Fellow members of High Country Writers have shared their collective and individual expertise and provided invaluable guidance in the preparation of this manuscript. I am honored to be among them. I am especially grateful to Marcia Cham and Sandy Horton for their assistance.

The wonderful people of the High Country have welcomed us and taught us so much about country life. I hope they know that we respect and admire them, even as we laugh at our clumsy adjustment to a completely different way of life in their mountains.

Finally, there would have been no Appalachian experience if my life partner had not said, "Let's do it," when we had the opportunity to purchase land in the lesbian and gay community, Happy Hollow, in the beautiful mountains of North Carolina. The warmth and encouragement she provided during the writing of this book made it a labor of love.

DEDICATION

To my only one, appropriately called Hope in these pages. At times I wonder if you are a figment of my imagination, but your constant love is a very real presence in my life. Thank you for introducing me to unconditional love and acceptance and your steadfast encouragement during the writing of this book.

INTRODUCTION

I knew as soon as the car left our concrete neighborhood and the first tree appeared on the horizon, my Dad would offer up his standard observation, "This is real country," cueing my brother and me to start appreciating trees, grass and anything else that reminded him of his boyhood days in the Blue Ridge Mountains of Virginia.

He must have tapped into the woodsy gene in each of us because we both ended up living in the mountains. In fact, I'd describe the area of Appalachia where I live as "extreme country." Fifty years later, we still break each other up when out of the blue, one of us repeats Dad's mantra, "This is real country."

We were never quite sure what distinguished a city park from real country. Both had trees and grass and even an occasional animal, so we figured it must have had something to do with distance from our home. Whatever it was, we both seemed destined to choose it over the city.

My brother came to it much earlier than I did as a member of the "back-to-the-land" group of twenty-somethings who packed up their Birkenstocks and headed for Vermont. While he was finding himself in the Green Mountains, I was fulfilling my role as the responsible oldest child by teaching high school history. He wanted to save the land; I set my sights on trying to save the world.

1

I believed urban America was where the action was. I could protest the Vietnam War, demonstrate for civil rights and reproductive freedom and do it all on national television. An eventual career shift to public relations consumed my time and energy so that I hardly noticed I was suffocating in a world of traffic, noise, political chaos and dirty air.

It seemed natural to consult the radio before leaving the house to find out which roads were clogged and where the safe detours were that would take me to my destination. No target was closer than an hour, even though the actual distance was in the single digits. I cannot imagine how many years I've spent in traffic, listening to the all news station on the car radio and using the program in my head to plot less congested escape routes. GPS gizmos had nothing on me when it came to finding alternates.

My reward for living this way was a series of good jobs with generous pay. Eventually, that financial benefit would be my ticket to real country.

Sometime during my fifth decade of city life I realized I needed to leave. When I looked at people in cars at traffic lights, I was alarmed at what I saw. They were tense, hostile to others around them, trying to cope with the over-stimulation of the urban circus. I began to see the blaring hip-hop and salsa music that rang out from cars in my neighborhood as an attempt to build a barrier between the drivers and the rest of the world.

Our home that had been an oasis in the middle of urban chaos had turned into a prison. The persistent sounds of sirens and whirring helicopters in a nightly search for criminals in our neighborhood robbed me of the peace I sought there. As I aged I lost confidence in my ability to outrun a mugger, so I didn't walk after dark or use mass transit. The cultural offerings of downtown Washington, D.C. began to lose their appeal when I contemplated the hassles of driving to them and finding a parking space.

Rush hour stretched from 5 a.m. until 10 or 11 a.m. and then started up again by 3:30 p.m. and went until 8 p.m. I was getting too tired to fight my way anywhere once I got home from work.

Meanwhile, that woodsy gene began sending me messages about getting away from the city to a calmer, greener place where

I could learn to relax. At the same time, my financial planner was suggesting I could retire at sixty-two. My mind kept returning to the confluence of these two messages as I thought about what I wanted to do with the rest of my life.

This city girl kept thinking about a simpler life in a log cabin in the mountains. I was searching for my inner Heidi. Fortunately, my partner had similar thoughts, and when an opportunity to purchase land in western North Carolina showed up on our radar screen, we jumped on it. For the next five years, we saved like crazy, imagining the log home we would build when I retired.

The decision was not without drama. When my partner, Hope, and I made a decision to purchase land in the mountains of western North Carolina and build a log home in Happy Hollow, a lesbian and gay community, our friends were skeptical. Skeptical is putting it mildly. "Are you crazy?" they demanded. "You're moving to the Bible Belt—to a gay and lesbian community?"

To understand their reaction, you need to know something about us. First, we are a lesbian couple who had lived all of our lives in urban areas. I grew up in Newark, New Jersey and Hope spent her formative years in northeastern Pennsylvania and Washington, D.C. When we committed ourselves to one another we moved into the very diverse, gay-friendly city of Takoma Park, Maryland, right outside Washington, D.C. where we lived for eighteen years.

Despite our urban backgrounds, we both loved the mountains and decided we wanted to spend the rest of our lives in a rural area, away from traffic congestion, inner city noise and pollution, and the stressful environment we'd lived in for too many years. We longed to be in a place where we could hear birds instead of sirens and maybe live a few years longer.

We brought with us a history of left-of-center politics and social and political activism, and knew it would be a challenge to reconcile that with an area that was home to some very conservative people. While not particularly observant, I've always identified as a Jew, and my partner, a former nun, is a self-described recovering Catholic.

We expected to spend some time in our new environment adjusting to a very different way of life. I was newly retired, and Hope planned to find a job doing something that would allow her to use her post-graduate education.

We moved into a rental house while our new log home was being constructed. Almost from the first day, we began to refer to our new surroundings as "The Holler," although we were not actually living in a holler at the time. Partly to maintain ties with friends around the country, I began a series of email letters or updates. The major purpose of those letters, however, was to ease my own adjustment to life in Appalachia and, as my ethnic heritage required, I had to do it with a large dose of humor. We Jews have always managed to find humor in life's challenges.

Now, three and a half years later, I find it hard to believe I ever chose to live anywhere else. Remembering our origins, my brother and I toasted our new log cabin in a predictable way. "This is real country," we said, and giggled over our herbal tea like a couple of kids in the back seat of our father's car.

Real Country is divided into two parts. Part I traces the events leading to our move to Appalachia. The second part consists of letters to friends. The response from friends to these letters is what made me decide to write this book. If you don't like it, feel free to blame them. I will.

Leslie Brunetsky
January 2009

PART I

- 1 -

Sick and Tired of City Life

"There's got to be a better way than this to live out my retirement," Leslie growled as she arrived home an hour and a half late due to yet another overturned eighteen-wheeler on the Washington Beltway. "Do you have any idea how many of our waking hours we spend in this rotten traffic?" she asked her life companion.

"I'm so tired of planning my life around traffic and accidents, hoping I'll be on time for appointments but knowing no matter how early I leave, I'll still run a fifty-fifty chance of being late. I'm sure there's an opportunity for a whole new art form in this—creative apologies for keeping people waiting."

"That's not even the worst part of living here," Hope chimed in. "I can't remember when I got a good nights' sleep with these damned sirens and helicopters waking me up every hour or more. Where the hell are these helicopters going at three and four in the morning anyway?"

"You know we're in the flight path between the White House and Camp David," Leslie reminded her. "Every time there's an incident anywhere in the world and the president is at his mountain retreat, the whirlybirds whisk him back to the White House. Then there's the MedEvac helipad for Washington Adventist Hospital around the corner that gets active whenever there's a serious accident nearby.

7

And of course, they use helicopters to chase criminals around the neighborhood. Sometimes I swear those chopper pilots buzz our roof to see how close they can get before our shingles fly off."

"I love this house," Hope sighed. Leslie could see the tears start to well up in her partner's eyes. She knew from experience they had arrived at the point when talk of leaving the area would usually get derailed and Hope would launch into a verbal catalogue of the wonderful memories they'd shared in this, their first house.

She could hardly believe what came out of Hope's mouth next. "... but as much as I love it I think we should start looking at other locations. After all, it's gotten so expensive to live here that we wouldn't be able to afford to stay in Maryland once you're no longer bringing in that big pay check. God knows we couldn't live on my salary, even with your pension and Social Security."

Leslie stared at Hope in disbelief. "Are you serious?"

"Let's get the atlas and pick some places to go see," Hope answered. Not wanting to waste the moment she'd been hoping for, Leslie fairly ran into the family room and pulled the Rand McNally atlas off the shelf. "Come on in here," she called to Hope. "Let's start a list of places."

That's how Leslie and Hope's journey from Takoma Park, Maryland to southern Appalachia began.

- 2 -

Log Cabin Fever

Though neither Leslie nor Hope had talked about it until fairly recently, it turned out that both shared a fantasy of living in a log cabin in the mountains. Hope's early years in the coal country of Pennsylvania's Pocono Mountains planted an appreciation of a slower, quieter pace of life. She had warm memories of hiking and fishing with her beloved Uncle John in those mountains and trips to visit cousins at nearby Lake Wallenpaupack.

Leslie recalled summer escapes from her family's Newark tenement to a Girl Scout camp in the Appalachian Mountains of northern New Jersey and college summers working in the Adirondack Mountains of New York. Those were among her happiest times.

The more they talked about moving to the mountains and building a log cabin, their excitement grew. Leslie tends to be practical, while Hope is more likely to follow her heart. These differences served them well as they began planning their future.

While Hope's mind raced off to selecting furniture for the cabin that would be their future home, Leslie started making lists. She made lists for everything. List number one: possible states to check out; List number two: log home builders; List number three: log home designs. And then there was the budget. What could they afford and how much did they need to save to realize this dream?

A couple of weekend trips to Pennsylvania and West Virginia to visit log home communities eliminated those states. The areas just didn't feel right. Both women had learned to trust their intuition about such things and had agreed beforehand that if an area didn't feel right, they would cross it off the list. That was how they'd chosen their first home and that worked well for eighteen years.

They spent two weeks one fall vacationing in the Adirondack Mountains and Vermont and decided winters there would be too cold as they got older. So far, they'd ruled out all of New England for weather reasons and Pennsylvania and West Virginia. Leslie was adamant about not moving to Virginia. "Too much bad karma there," she told Hope. "That's where my father's family was from and I really don't want to get planted anywhere near those roots." They agreed to scratch Virginia from the list.

During a weekend visit to friends Janis and Kay at Smith Mountain Lake, Kay mentioned they'd heard of a gay and lesbian log home community being developed somewhere in the mountains of North Carolina. Until their friends mentioned it, Hope and Leslie hadn't given any thought to a lifestyle community, probably because they didn't even know such places existed. Kay gave Leslie and Hope the name of the developers and they said they'd call them when they got home.

Driving back to Maryland, they talked about this new concept and warmed to the notion. The idea of having a community of like-minded people who would respect their relationship and provide support as they aged was appealing. But they knew nothing about western North Carolina except what they'd gleaned from a long weekend in Asheville several years earlier.

A quick call to developers Geri and Chris the next day provided some interesting information. These women had developed a gay and lesbian community in Florida and were now looking for land in the western North Carolina mountains to build a similar community, but with log homes. They told Leslie and Hope they were close to selecting a piece of property and explained the process by which people could reserve a place in line to purchase a lot at

Happy Hollow.

Hope didn't take long to make her mind up. "Let's do it." she said. Leslie was not quite ready to make a commitment to purchase land she hadn't seen and there were other considerations to think about. "From Geri and Chris' description of where this community will be, it sounds like it's right in the middle of the Bible Belt," she reminded Hope. "I'm not sure how welcome a gay community will be there. Besides, North Carolina is a red state and we're anything but red. I'm not sure I could stand having Jesse Helms representing me in the U.S. Senate."

From what Geri and Chris had said, it would be several months before any lots would be available in the new development. Leslie and Hope decided they would take their next vacation in the area and see how it felt. It wouldn't hurt to get their names on the waiting list in case they decided they liked the area, so they sent a refundable deposit to the developers.

A few months later they heard from Geri and Chris that they'd purchased one hundred eighty acres of land in the North Carolina Mountains. They estimated it would take at least four months until they were ready to sell lots. That gave Hope and Leslie time to check the area out.

Some folks believe the area around Boone, North Carolina is a vortex of energy. Others are drawn to it for skiing and cool summers. Maybe it was a coincidence that Leslie and Hope drove into town from the eastern side and immediately saw a rainbow sign on the Unitarian Universalist church, a symbol that gays are welcome. Perhaps it had more to do with women they met in Boone through mutual friends. Everything they saw and heard during their two weeks in the area was appealing. They fell in love with it.

They spent time exploring the area and hiked into the property that was being developed into Happy Hollow. By the time they drove back to Maryland they had decided they would purchase a lot in the new development and build their log cabin once Leslie retired.

How in the world would two flatlanders from the city select the right mountain lot to build a log cabin? They realized picking the wrong lot could be an expensive mistake, so they hired a local architect who knew the area. They gave him a rough idea of the type of house they wanted to build, all on one level with a garage beneath and a view of the mountains. Leslie was adamant about the view. "If I'm going to live in the mountains," she told Hope, "I want to be able to look out my windows and see mountains. Otherwise, I could live anywhere and watch mountains on the Weather Channel." Hope agreed that was an important consideration.

They kept track of the progress at Happy Hollow and visited while the roads were being constructed. There was a rough map of where lots in the first section would be and they went to look over the area with Dwayne, their architect. They asked him to keep checking on the land and recommend a lot that would meet their needs.

Armed with topographic maps and the developers' description of the potential lots, they chose the one they thought would work best for the house they planned to build. They wondered what Dwayne would come up with. Meanwhile, as the road work continued they started talking to log home companies. They began what was to be a lengthy education on log home construction.

Dwayne sent them his lot recommendations and they were elated to see that he had selected the same one they had as his first choice for them. "That does it," Leslie told Hope. "Since Dwayne chose the same lot we did, that's the one we'll buy."

"But what if somebody else picks it first?" Hope asked. They pored over maps and considered Dwayne's second and third choices and decided that Lot 16 was the only one they wanted. If they couldn't have that one, they'd pass on choosing a lot in the first section.

They nervously awaited a call from Chris and Geri asking for their choice of lot. By prearrangement, they knew they would have 24 hours to make a decision once they got the phone call. They also knew there were eighteen people ahead of them in the queue to choose a lot.

They received a letter saying the lot selection had begun and they should expect a call in a couple of weeks. To their surprise, less than a week later Chris called and asked if they had a choice. "We want Lot 16," Leslie told her.

"What's your second choice?" Chris asked. "We don't have one. It's Lot 16 or none," Leslie replied. She held her breath and was disappointed when Chris told her somebody had a "hold" on Lot 16. "I thought nobody could put a 'hold' on lots," Leslie said. Chris said that she'd call the women who put the hold on Lot 16 and tell them they had to make a decision. "What if you can't reach them?" Leslie asked, mindful of their 24-hour time limit. "I'll give them until tomorrow morning to get back to me," Chris said, "and if I don't hear from them by noon tomorrow, the lot is yours."

Leslie and Hope left for work the next morning with more than a little anxiety. Leslie had a tight meeting schedule for most of the day and wondered if she'd hear from Chris at work. She didn't. When she got home, she checked the message machine and saw a blinking red light.

She was dying to listen to the message but wanted Hope to hear it too, so she waited. "Damned traffic," she fumed. Hope said she'd be home on time but Leslie knew she was probably tied up in traffic. Route 95 South was always a mess during the evening rush hour. She knew it was useless to call Hope's cell phone since Hope almost never remembered to keep it on. "Maybe the message isn't even from them," she said to herself. "It could be anybody."

Leslie moved around the kitchen as if in slow motion. Every minute seemed like an hour as she started supper preparations. The blinking red light on the answering machine on the kitchen counter took over the room. Finally, after what seemed an eternity, she heard Hope's key in the front door.

Before Hope got as far as the kitchen she called out, "Did she call you?" "No, but there's a message on our machine," Leslie answered. "Well, what did it say?" Hope asked. "I don't know. I didn't listen to it," Leslie replied. "I wanted us to listen together."

Hope put her briefcase down and walked over to Leslie. "If it's meant to be, it will happen," she said as she reached out for a hug. "I can't stand this another minute. Let's listen to it," and she pressed the message button on the machine.

A flat nasal voice said, "Hi ladies. This is Chris letting you know Lot 16 is yours! Congratulations. Give me a call when you get this and we can talk about the closing details. Welcome to

Happy Hollow."

"Play it again," said Hope. "This is a voice from our future."

- 3 -

Hurry Up and Wait

"How are we ever going to get through the next five years?" Leslie wondered over supper. "That's the soonest I can retire." "It's going to seem like an eternity," Hope said, "but when I think of leaving our house and our friends I feel really sad. And my job, I just started it and I'll have to leave it." Leslie took a deep breath and reminded Hope that she'd been the one to want to jump at the opportunity to buy the land in North Carolina. "I know, I know, but now that it's a reality, I'm scared," Hope said. Leslie admitted to being a little scared too but quickly shifted into talking about the future as she'd done through her entire life.

"We're doing this together and it's not as if we have to give up our friends. You just wait and see. They'll all want to visit us when the summer temperatures here hit the ninety-degree mark and they can't breathe in this lousy humidity," she told Hope.

Leslie reflected that Hope had come a long way from the days after they first bought their house. She reminded Hope how homesick she'd been when they went to Cape May with friends for a long weekend not long after moving to Takoma Park. "Remember the time when I went for bagels for breakfast and came back to the motel to find you standing, staring out the window with tears running down your face? When I asked you what was wrong, you said you missed our house and were just thinking how the sunlight

15

reflected through the window on the second floor landing." "Don't talk about that or you'll make me cry," Hope said. "You know how I love this house."

By unspoken agreement they knew Leslie would have to be the one to tell friends of their decision. The first opportunity came within the week when they were hosting a dinner party to celebrate Hope's birthday. They'd been celebrating birthdays with Deb and Joanne and Yvonne and Lois for years. The dynamic that developed when the three couples got together was something special, a real warmth and enjoyment of being together. They laughed so hard that somebody always ended up dashing away from the table to the nearest bathroom. Leslie waited until they were eating birthday cake to announce their purchase of the North Carolina property.

Their friends knew they'd been exploring the possibility of buying land and eventually moving there but it hadn't seemed real until now. "Congratulations," Joanne said. You could feel the tension around the table. "Tell us about it," said Yvonne. Leslie and Hope explained how they'd chosen their lot and how they'd be saving for the next five years until Leslie could retire, avoiding the obvious part about leaving Maryland.

Then the questions started. "Are you sure you'll be safe down there? That's Klan country, isn't it? You'll be surrounded by very conservative people in Appalachia." And so it went. One by one, Hope and Leslie addressed their questions and tried to explain that the area was different from what they'd heard. They told how Chris and Geri had personally gone to every house near Happy Hollow and talked with the residents about the type of community they were developing and that they intended to be good neighbors. The neighbors were polite and cordial.

No matter how much Leslie tried to convince their friends that the presence of a university in Boone changed the character of the immediate area, it didn't make much of a dent in their wary response to the news. Everybody around the table knew the real issue was that they were unhappy that Leslie and Hope would be leaving Maryland.

Telling other friends was not easy either. Most had pretty much the same reaction, thinking Hope and Leslie were crazy to move to an area thought to be hostile to outsiders, particularly gay Yankees.

Leslie wasn't sure how Hope would react when the time actually came to leave the Takoma Park house and their friends. She was going to have to work to keep the reality of it in the foreground so that Hope would start to come to terms with it before five years were up.

Taking the wall calendar down, Leslie started counting the months until they would move to North Carolina. She put a number on each page to correspond to the total of months left until her retirement. For the next five years, each time a new month started, Hope would make the same comment when she saw the number of months left before their move to North Carolina. "Do you have to do this?" she asked Leslie. "Yes, I do. Some months looking at that number is the only way I can cope with the stress of my job. As long as the number decreases, I feel I can hang on."

There was a lot of work to do before they could build their log cabin. For the next few years they spent weekends attending log home shows, perusing *Log Home Living* magazines and looking at home designs on the Internet. What they lacked in expertise they more than made up for in diligent pursuit of knowledge about log homes.

They went to workshops and read everything they could find about choosing a log home company. Just when they had decided on a company, they heard about another one that sounded better. There were loads of opinions about whether to go with a national firm or a local one, depending on who you talked to. 'So many decisions to make.

During one trip to look at their land, they were scheduled to meet with Nicole, vice president of her family's log home company. They arranged to meet at a ramshackle old grocery store in the middle of nowhere so she could show them some homes her company had built. They'd had several phone conversations with her and knew she was fairly young but when she jumped out of her jeep to greet them, they were sure they'd made a mistake. Nicole, in her thirties at the time, was wearing short shorts and a skimpy top and looked to be 18 years old. "God, it's Daisy Mae," Leslie whispered to Hope under her breath. "This will be quick."

Within half an hour their impression changed and Hope and Leslie were convinced that Nicole knew her business. She'd grown up with her parents' log home company and, as they later learned, was highly respected among builders, vendors and other contractors. Everything they'd read and heard about choosing a log home company cautioned that the clients had to feel comfortable with the people. Once back in Maryland, they were pretty sure they wanted to work with her company.

They had several phone conversations with Nicole over the next couple of years and by the time they were ready to have house plans drawn, they knew she was the one they wanted for their contractor. During one of their visits to North Carolina she and one of her builders looked at their lot and agreed that they'd chosen well for the design they wanted. That was a relief.

Meanwhile, their plans took an unexpected turn. A dear elderly neighbor of theirs, Sara, started having health problems. She ended up in a nursing home until a friend invited her to move in with her family in Tennessee. One day Leslie received a phone call from Sara's friend, Theresa, saying she didn't want them to worry if they saw people carrying things out of Sara's house. Theresa had sold it. When she told Leslie how much she'd sold it for, Leslie couldn't believe it. Sara's house was smaller than theirs and hadn't had any improvements made since the house was built in the early 1950's. Much as they loved Sara, they recognized that housekeeping was not her strong suit. The house was a mess.

Leslie and Hope had intended to put their house up for sale six months before they planned to move to North Carolina and had not even been taking note of home prices in their neighborhood. Leslie was still two years away from retirement and had planned to take advantage of being mortgage free for a couple of years to save for their log cabin.

Hope returned from doing errands a short while after the conversation with Theresa and Leslie greeted her with the news about Sara's house. "Guess what they sold it for," Leslie said. When she told Hope the selling price, without skipping a beat Hope said, "Call the realtor."

"You're kidding, right?" Leslie asked. "No, I'm not." Hope replied. "Let's find out what our house is worth." Leslie picked up the phone and called the realtor who had sold Sara's house and made an appointment for the woman to come and give them a price that afternoon.

Within two days, they'd met with two realtors and had been given identical prices for their house. This was a momentous decision to consider, to sell and move to a rental house for two years, or to stay put and hope the real estate market would not collapse before they were ready to sell. It called for a consultation with their financial planner. Things were happening at head-spinning speed and they feared trusting their own judgment.

The timing for the decision to sell or stay wasn't the best. To celebrate their 20th anniversary, Leslie and Hope were going to Italy for three weeks and they were also due in Detroit for a weekend visit to Hope's family in a couple of weeks. But they managed to get an appointment with their financial planner within a couple of days.

She ran the numbers and advised them to sell their house while the market was hot. She said they could rent another house for two years and still have enough money to build their log cabin when Leslie retired. Besides, it would be a lot easier to move to North Carolina if they didn't have to wait around to sell, she told them. They'd worked with Merle for several years and had confidence in her but she never pressed them to take her advice; she always said they should think about it. During their drive home from the meeting they weighed the pros and cons of following her advice. Hope's commute was intolerable, sometimes taking over two hours. If they moved to Columbia, Maryland it would shave off about an hour of driving time to Baltimore for her and the change in Leslie's commute to Annapolis would be negligible.

The other big plus about moving to Columbia was that four of their closest friends lived there. Leslie wondered if she could adapt to such a suburban environment, even for two years. She'd always made fun of Columbia's "phony neighborhoods," as she called them. Columbia, Maryland was one of the first planned communities that consisted of a series of villages, each with a small town center, and while she applauded the concept, it always seemed like a very artificial place.

The prospect of a shorter commute for Hope outweighed any reservations about living in a fake town, so they decided to sell the Takoma Park house. They called Gail, the realtor who seemed most likely to bring good results, and placed the house on the market. She told them they didn't need to do a thing to prepare the house for sale; it was perfect the way it was. Hope baked an apple pie the morning of the first open house so the place would smell of cinnamon, her idea of an irresistible, homey aroma.

Nine days later, while Hope and Leslie were in Detroit visiting family, Gail called saying she had an offer on the house. It met the asking price and the prospective buyer's financial information checked out, so they gave her the go ahead. It was getting to be Pepto Bismol time, a term they used to describe a favorite tool for dealing with too much excitement.

They returned to Maryland for one week and then left for Italy, knowing they'd have about three weeks when they returned to find a place to rent in Columbia, pack up the house, and move. No matter, the trip to Italy had been planned for over a year and there was no way they'd consider postponing it. Off they went, Leslie fortifying herself with a mega dose of Dramamine and Hope with Tylenol PM for the long flight.

- 4 -

Two Farewells

Italy was wonderful. Leslie and Hope actually managed to forget about moving and finding a place to live while they soaked up the culture of Rome, Florence and Venice. Leslie had been to Italy a couple of times and was able to serve as a tour guide for Hope, something they both preferred to being herded around on a bus.

As an added bonus, they met Leslie's English cousin, Stuart, and his wife Margaret for a delightful evening in Florence. It turned out to be an anniversary trip for them as well. A side trip to Assisi to walk in the footsteps of St. Francis was special to Hope who had spent five years in a Franciscan convent.

When it was time to leave Italy, the women had predictable reactions. After twenty years of vacationing together, it was a safe bet Leslie wanted to stay for a few more weeks and Hope was getting homesick. They said "Arrivederci" to Italy and flew back to reality in Maryland, knowing the next farewell would not be as easy.

Back home, the fun was about to begin. The realtor had set a closing date for the sale of their house and they had three weeks to find a rental house, pack up eighteen years of accumulated contents of their home, find a mover, and relocate to Columbia. The packing began in earnest as soon as they got back from Italy.

Fortunately, they found a house to rent within two days. It was bigger than they needed but they wouldn't have to put any of their furniture in storage. They signed a two-year lease, knowing they'd be moving to North Carolina the day the lease expired. A friend recommended a reliable and affordable mover and they set the move date for the day before the closing on the house. They were warned that closings can get postponed or cancelled and knew they were taking a chance that everything might not go as scheduled, but things had been working so smoothly they figured their luck would continue.

For the next few weeks, every waking moment that wasn't spent at their jobs, they packed. Friends helped pack and ferry belongings to the rental house in Columbia.

It was such a blur that even Hope didn't really have much time to get too upset about leaving their home. There were times, though, when she would suddenly find a photo or knick knack that made her stop and get teary.

It wasn't going to be easy to leave this house that held so many memories for them. "You know that wherever we are together, even if it's a cave or a tent, will be home," Leslie would tell her. "We're what makes a house a home." And then after a comforting hug, the packing would resume.

Finally, moving day arrived and the women made several trips back and forth to Columbia to supervise the movers and transport items they didn't trust the movers to carry. It was a long day but things went smoothly. They had arranged to move on Saturday so they'd have Sunday to get things unpacked and arranged.

Monday was closing day on the Takoma Park house. Leslie planned to take the whole day off to do the final walk-through with the new buyers in the morning. Hope was afraid she'd cry and didn't want to do that in front of strangers. She would join Leslie in the afternoon for the closing.

The first snafu of the day occurred when the buyer failed to show for the morning walk-through. Gail assured Leslie they could still do the closing that afternoon. At 1 p.m. they met Gail for a cup of coffee to discuss last-minute details about the closing that was scheduled for 2 p.m. They knew from the look on her face that something was amiss. "The lawyer for the buyers called to say he's running behind and he has to put the closing off until 3:30," she told them. She left to cancel a couple of appointments so she could make the change and said she'd see them later.

At 3:30 Leslie and Hope showed up at the office where the lawyer was to meet them and told the receptionist why they were there. She knew nothing about the closing so she called the lawyer and he said he expected them to meet at another location, half an hour's drive from where they were. By this time it was rush hour and they were in no mood to fight traffic. Leslie took the phone from the receptionist and asked the lawyer why he didn't tell their realtor about the changed location. He did the wrong thing at that moment; he laughed and said, "What's your problem?"

Leslie let all of the pent-up tension of the day fly in his direction. "Look," she told him, "you're the one with the problem. We don't have to sell this house today or any day for that matter. And we don't have to sell it to your clients at all." Gail walked into the office, just in time to hear Leslie tell the lawyer, "We are where we were told to be and if your clients want to buy this house, you and they need to get over here or we're leaving."

By this time, Hope was staring wide-eyed at Leslie, wondering what the lawyer had said to set her off. Leslie gave the phone back to the receptionist and told Hope and Gail what the lawyer had said. "Calm down," Hope said. "We're very stressed out and we do want to sell this house today." "Yes, we do want to do that," chimed in the realtor, who didn't want to see her commission evaporate. "These things happen all the time. You'll see; it will be OK." she continued.

The lawyer and his clients showed up forty minutes later and the closing process began. What took place over the next couple of hours was like a bad movie. The cast of characters truly represented the diversity that was typical of Takoma Park.

The man to whom they were selling the house was a middle-aged white guy. He showed up stoned, which might account for the inappropriate comments he made throughout the meeting. His fiancée was a Malaysian woman whose English was limited. She was represented by a Vietnamese realtor whose English was hard to understand, and the fiancée's brother was acting as interpreter for the realtor and his sister. The lawyer was from Ghana and had a most annoying habit of giggling every time he spoke.

Gail signed all the papers she had to sign and then left. At that point, Leslie told the lawyer she needed a break and she and Hope stepped out of the office.

"Do you think we're on Candid Camera?" Hope asked as soon as they were out of earshot. "If we are, the viewers must be laughing their asses off," Leslie replied. "Our buyer is obviously stoned and his fiancée doesn't seem to understand anything that's going on and I have no clue what the brother is translating to the other realtor," she went on. "Gail seemed to think everything was in order or she wouldn't have left, I'm sure, so let's just get this over with and get out of here. I wonder if the lawyer is on dope too. He obviously sees something funny that we don't."

Two hours later, the papers were all signed and the lawyer started packing up his briefcase. The stoned buyer asked if Leslie and Hope would be willing to go to the house with him and show him how to work the hot tub. Only somebody with impaired judgment would have asked that question. "You had your chance," Hope snapped. "If you had shown up for the walk-through this morning, you would have received an explanation."

Leslie was stunned at Hope's response. So was the new owner. She knew it took a lot to get Hope angry enough to confront someone and figured she'd better get her out of there before it turned really ugly. She tried to steer Hope toward the door but wasn't fast enough. "Look it up on the Internet if you can figure out how to do it," Hope continued. She really knew how to hurt the guy; he was a computer engineer.

Hope stormed out of the office and Leslie followed. Once in the car and a safe distance away from the scene of the closing comedy, Hope told Leslie, "I feel badly about what I did but when I saw the look on your face when he asked us to go show him how to work the hot tub I was afraid you'd kill him, so I jumped in."

"Actually, I knew the house belonged to him at that point," Leslie said, "so I didn't give a damn. He'll probably have to pay somebody to show him and it's his own fault." They laughed and expressed relief that the whole ridiculous scene was over as they drove to their new, temporary home in Columbia.

It was a few days before Hope confided to Leslie one evening over dinner how much she missed their house. "I know you do," Leslie said. "I do too, but now we have to start thinking about our new house in North Carolina." She took out the blueprints of their log cabin and they spent the rest of the evening planning their future home.

The two years in Columbia passed quickly and were bearable because they got to spend much more time with their good friends who lived there. Leslie got over the discomfort of living in an artificial town as the months wound down to her retirement and Hope was relieved to spend two hours a day commuting instead of four.

- 5 -

Heading for the Hills

After five years of looking longingly at the photo of the North Carolina mountains on her desk at work, Leslie announced she would retire from her job in two months. Hope also gave notice at her job and they began a round of bittersweet farewells at home and at work.

They'd gotten pretty good at packing and it went faster this time. They'd been buying light fixtures, carpets and other items for their new home, so that added to the volume. They called Nick, the mover who'd moved them to Columbia, and he agreed to move them to North Carolina.

Nicole said it would take about a year for her to build their home at Happy Hollow and they were lucky to find a great rental house in West Jefferson, forty minutes away from the Hollow. Things were falling into place nicely and the excitement was building toward moving day on June 10th.

It took Nick and the boys nearly all day to pack two trucks. The plan was for them to start the trip, spend the night somewhere in Virginia, and then drive to West Jefferson the next day. Leslie and Hope stayed to clean the house before dropping off the keys at the rental agent's office. By the time they started the drive to North Carolina with two cars packed to capacity, it was rush hour in the Washington, D.C. area. They were tired and anxious to get on the road but nobody and nothing moves during rush hour around Washington.

They spent a couple of hours in northern Virginia sitting in bumper-to-bumper gridlock and finally decided to stop for dinner and wait it out.

Their friends Lee and Heather had given them a set of walkie-talkies so they could communicate during the long drive, knowing cell phones wouldn't work well once they got into the Blue Ridge Mountains. That gift was a lifesaver, literally. If they'd not been able to keep a running conversation, fatigue might have gotten the better of them.

Leslie's night blindness made the drive after dark difficult and exhausting and when rain began shortly after they crossed the North Carolina border, she told Hope she needed to stop and catch a quick nap. They pulled off and found a gas station parking lot and Leslie slept for an hour while Hope, parked alongside her car, stood guard. She was too wired to sleep. By the time Leslie awoke the rain had stopped and they finished the remaining three hours of the trip.

At 4 a.m., twelve hours after leaving Columbia, Maryland they arrived at the house that would be their home for the next 11 months. "We made it!" they said nearly simultaneously as they got out of their cars.

The house was tucked away in a rural area and they assumed nothing was open, but they were delighted to discover an all-night coffee shop nearby. They had run out of food about four hours into the trip they had estimated would take seven hours. It was a tossup which need was stronger, the one for food or sleep. Food won out and they had a quick breakfast before settling down to sleep on the floor of their temporary home. They fantasized about sleeping in their own bed the next night and drifted off for a few hours' sleep, tired but very happy to be in the mountains.

PART II

Settling in to their new rural life required lots of adjusting for Leslie and Hope. It was the first time either of them was living in a culture that was so different from what they knew. While helpful and friendly, their new neighbors wasted little time letting them know they were foreigners, a term they first thought was cute but later suspected wasn't always meant in the nicest way.

Leslie's letters to friends were intended to help ease their transition and also to let friends know they were enjoying mountain life. As people often do, Leslie and Hope used humor to mask their initial discomfort as they tried to fit into the culture of the mountains. West Jefferson was a long way from Washington, D.C. and a world away from the Northeast where they had both been raised.

- 1 -

New Tarheels

June 18, 2005

Dear Friends,

Well, here we are in the Tarheel State, a bit worn at the heels from the moving and subsequent unpacking, but happy to be in such a beautiful place. As of yesterday, our rented house is starting to look more like a home and less like a Costco warehouse after a riot.

It's been quite a full week since our 4 a.m. arrival last Saturday, and we are enjoying the natural beauty of our mountain surroundings. We are located in a delightful, tranquil setting across the road from a Christmas tree farm. We look out the window at a cow pasture with real cows slightly up the mountain to our left and only three other houses. The view of Mt. Jefferson from the front windows is framed by mostly blue sky and evergreens. How could anyone not like this place?

Considering our short time here, we've already begun to develop a social life. Two new friends, Dottie and Lyn, future neighbors at Happy Hollow, brought us a cooked dinner on Sunday after our arrival and forced us to sit down and relax. Of course, with only two to three hours of sleep, and those spent semi-conscious on a quilt on the floor, relaxing was pretty easy. We managed to remain upright in our chairs and apparently didn't do or say anything outlandish, because we've seen them a few times since then. Come to think of it, since they're from Fire Island, NY, it would probably be pretty hard to do something outrageous by their standards.

We have registered to vote, probably sending shock waves through this Republican district. Hope is convinced that we'll never get our voter registration cards because they don't want Democrats voting here.

After taking a written test, we both now have NC driver's licenses. I would have flunked the test if a guy hadn't come in to plead with the state trooper to get his license back. He'd refused to take a breathalyzer test and lost it. They don't fool around with DWI incidents here. Anyway, I was eavesdropping, and it was a good thing. Had I not done so, I'd have missed two questions on the test and failed. Hope benefited from my nosiness, and armed with my notes, took the test the next day and passed with flying colors.

We're beginning to get used to satellite TV; I only called tech support three times so far. We're also getting comfortable taking our trash to the dump, since there's no pickup service here. It makes me long for the good old days when I just tossed stuff into an incinerator chute and left the rest to the super. Depositing garbage is quite complicated. I'm sure we broke some of the recycling rules, but we're learning.

We have three supermarkets within five miles of our house and have already figured out which are the best. To my considerable shock, one even has a kosher foods section. Someone must have tipped them off that I was coming.

We now have a built-in excuse for whatever culinary goofs occur in our kitchen—the high altitude. Since neither of us did particularly well in physics, we don't know exactly why foods cook faster or more slowly, but whatever goes wrong, we are blaming on the 3,000 foot altitude. These things never happened at sea level.

We have also broadened our argument repertoire. Now we can argue over whether the red flag on the mailbox goes up before the letter carrier comes, or whether he puts it up. I'm insisting we leave the flag down, and he puts it up to let us know we have mail. Hope says we put the flag up to let him know there's outgoing mail, and he puts it down to let us know it's been picked up. Five dollars are riding on this one.

Life was simpler when the mail was pushed through the slot in our front door. Of course we didn't get any exercise that way either. Here, I have to hike up and down a steep gravel driveway to get the mail. My goal is to be able to do that without getting winded by the time we move.

On Wednesday our brother Barry and nephew Elijah will arrive from Vermont and we're hoping to have sheets on the bed. With any luck, they won't have to climb over too much to get to the bathroom. We're also hoping that the landlord will have hired an exterminator to get rid of our unexpected roommates.

We're still trying to get used to the absence of sirens and the sounds of whirring helicopters searching for criminals at night. As a result, our sleeping has not been great. When we finally did get to sleep one night, I was sure I heard someone trying to break into the house. A quick tour of the house with a flashlight confirmed that there were mice in the attic, where we have most of our furniture and artwork stored. Those suckers are a damned sight noisier than city roaches.

A friend suggested we put sheets of fabric softener around because mice don't like it. It seems to work, but we want a more permanent solution to the problem. Besides, it makes the attic smell like a Mafia funeral.

On a more mundane note, Hope plans to ratchet up the job search next week. I am thoroughly enjoying being retired and living in the mountains. It's like stepping into a Heidi movie. You'll have to come visit us to see what we mean. We promise clean sheets, good food and a relaxing environment.

Peace and Love,
Leslie and Hope

June 26, 2005

Dear Friends,

Now that we've been Tarheels for two weeks, the place is starting to feel like home. We're fully licensed, registered to vote, and have NC plates on both cars. 'Can't get much more official than that. Oh yes, we've paid the highway use taxes too, so we're now pulling our weight alongside the mountaineers.

Barry and Elijah visited for three days and we found it easy to entertain in beautiful weather. We took them to Trade Days, a local event just over the Tennessee border, expecting to soak up some local culture. We were disappointed to see the same funnel cakes, pizza, Chinese food, etc. that we'd seen at fairs in Maryland. Isn't it wonderful that the fine things in life are so universal?

We took in opening night of *The Sound of Music*, performed by our local theater group. That calls for full dress here, clean jeans. We were pleasantly surprised that such a small community should have so many people with great voices. Hope was a bit chagrined that the nuns all wore different habits, a definite goof according to her, and one that would never be tolerated in any convent.

During intermission, we chatted with a local guy who just opened up a hair styling salon. He encouraged us to come in, so we decided that we'll send Hope for the first haircut. She has to look good for job interviews, and I don't have to look good for anything now. Just about any hair style goes with jeans and T-shirts.

Once the boys left, we went to a brunch with about forty retired women where we learned about an upcoming Boone Gay Pride party, the first ever. Imagine that! We will definitely go to support the cause. Be ready with bail money.

We're eagerly anticipating Christmas in July in our little town of West Jefferson. It's a huge event that draws thousands into this town of twelve hundred people. They say it's not to be missed because the mountain people come down for it and the sights are worth seeing. We couldn't miss the opportunity to meet some of the families who have inhabited Ashe County for centuries. I'm sure we'll look interesting to them too.

Thanks to those who replied about the flag on the mailbox. The letter carrier also kicked in with advice in the form of a note telling us not to put the flag up unless we have mail to be picked up. Hope won $5 on that one and is still wearing a smirk. I, on the other hand, am being gracious in defeat.

Hope to hear from you soon.

Peace and Love,
Leslie and Hope

July 3, 2005

Dear Friends,

It's surely not news to anyone that there is quite a bit of religion in the holler. I think there must be at least one Baptist church for every three people. Therefore, I was not surprised Monday morning when I approached our local supermarket (American owned, it says on the sign) and saw a group of elderly people sitting at tables in the cafe with their heads bowed. The cafe is where old folks go to get incredibly cheap meals. I figured they were saying grace, but they never lifted their heads.

As I got close enough to see the tables I realized they were staring intently at Bingo cards. Yes, another cultural offering in the holler, Monday morning supermarket Bingo. I could hear the caller shouting, and I do mean shouting, out the numbers with a pronounced New York accent. Probably because of his accent, there was an echo following each call, a translation if you will, by a woman with a local holler accent. The scene was just too funny. I've never had so much fun shopping for food.

We had a computer mishap this week; we couldn't access our documents. This posed a huge problem for Hope in her job search, so, not knowing anyone, I called the first number I found in the phone book for computer repair and told the guy what was happening. He said we'd have to bring the computer to his shop and I told him I was too old to do that. He said he'd make a house call and was here two hours later.

Tom, the computer guy, spent about an hour here doing all sorts of diagnostics and never batted an eye at the desktop photo of us arm-in-arm at the entrance to Happy Hollow. He ended up taking the computer to his shop to work on it, promising he'd have it back the next day.

The next day he actually called to say he'd bring it back that afternoon. Imagine that! Meanwhile, I was unpacking and working around the house and listening to some old Joan Baez CDs. When he walked in with the computer, guess what was playing. None other than "The Night They Drove Old Dixie Down," and I was mortified. I started talking to him nonstop, hoping he wouldn't hear the music. If that wasn't enough to insult him, when we opened my e-mail to be sure it was all there, up popped a message from an old NC friend with the subject line, "Are you a mountain hillbilly yet?" Tom and I laughed at that, but I could just see the price of the repair going up with every insult. First Joan Baez rubbing salt in the Civil War wound, and now this! Four hours of labor, two house calls, friendly service, and I nearly dropped when he told me the price—$100. Life here in the holler is good—and cheap. Come on down.

The much-heralded Christmas in July arrived and on a beastly hot day we took in the sights with some of our new Happy Hollow neighbors-to-be. The Republicans and Democrats were out distributing fans and when one of our friends gave the Dems a $20 donation, they were so excited they nearly kissed her. You'd have thought she gave them $10,000. Republicans outnumber Democrats and there's not much money among the locals, so hers was considered a major contribution. As everyone knows, in my native New Jersey corruption in city politics runs rampant. You would think we could buy favors from public officials here for a lot less, but I suspect kinship carries a bit more leverage than money.

For us, the highlight of Christmas in July was spotting a vendor's truck that read, "Tied Up with Jesus," figuring that there must be a Christian S & M group around here. One of our new friends, a former nun, found that a hopeful sign. As it turns out, they were selling ties and scarves with a Christian theme. I'm sure they haven't a clue how some folks might interpret their name.

That's about it from the holler. Happy Independence Day! Keep those cards and letters coming.

Peace and Love,
Leslie and Hope

July 10, 2005

Dear Friends,

We continue to try to figure out the culture of the holler. We recently learned about one small bit of driving etiquette that has to do with raising one's finger. No, not that finger. Unlike what we were used to in the D.C. area, where you usually saw people giving you the finger in your rear view mirror, people here raise their index finger as they're approaching you.

At first, we were understandably confused, wondering what we'd done wrong. We figured they didn't like our out-of-state tags, but it continued after we got NC tags. Then we thought they, like my late mother, didn't know which finger to use.

We've since learned that it's a friendly greeting. You simply raise your index finger of the hand that is gripping the top of the steering wheel, as a way of saying "Howdy neighbor." It's rather nice when you're driving out on a lonely, curvy mountain road to get a friendly greeting from a stranger, even if they are taking their half of the road out of the middle. I'm glad we got that straightened out; we were starting to get paranoid.

The supermarket continues to be a source of inexpensive entertainment for us. The other day we were reviewing the seafood and saw fresh squid. We asked the young man behind the counter to give us some, and watched with amusement as he barely managed to suppress his gag reflex. We guessed he wasn't as familiar with squid as he probably is with some other type of local delicacies. He had on vinyl gloves, and like a real trooper, managed to get the slimy stuff in the bag without retching.

We've begun to appreciate the differences between the work ethic of the holler as compared with the one we were used to "up Nawth." Here, people work to live, as opposed to some "Nawtheners" who live to work. You can tell by the hours they work.

On the surface, it seemed to us that they worked just enough to earn the money to pay the bills and then stopped, but we've recently learned that many of them go home from their day jobs and put in another four or five hours working on their farms.

We got a taste of the limited daytime hours when we went car shopping on Saturday afternoon. We knew we needed a four-wheel drive vehicle for the holler winters. We had plans to meet friends for dinner in Boone and figured we'd hit a couple of car dealerships first. At 5:15 we pulled into a Subaru dealer and things looked strangely quiet. We looked around for a quarantine sign or something to account for the absence of people. Nothing. Not being slaves to brand loyalty, we drove to the Toyota dealer. Same story.

After talking with some neighbors, we realized that people here like to spend time with their families. Imagine that. They also like to go fishing and hunting and sometimes, they just like to sit on the porch and rock.

Unlike the maniacs in some parts of the country (and us in our former lives) they see no need to work sixty to seventy hours a week at their day jobs. As a result, most businesses here close by 5 or 6 p.m. Since you don't find too many workaholics here, very few stores stay open until 10:00 or later to accommodate them. Incidentally, people seem to live longer here too. I think they've figured out something we've yet to learn.

Well, with a scant four weeks under our belts as residents of the holler, we've done it. We made High Country history last night. And no, we weren't arrested. We attended the first ever Boone Pride Party complete with loud music and North Carolina's most famous drag queen, Jamie. Happy Hollow was one of the sponsors, so we went to show our support. They had promised an hour of oldies music, but after a couple of dances, we "oldies" had to catch our breath and take a break from the volume, and sought refuge in the hallway.

From our hallway vantage point we were able to watch the police officer who had been sent to guard us. 'Poor guy must have drawn the short straw that night. You should have seen his face when Jamie, resplendent in pink chiffon and feathers, got ready to make her entrance. Jamie was primping in the hall, and this guy had a look on his face that was priceless. It was well worth the price of admission and then some.

We know you're all wondering about the progress on our log

home. So are we. The equipment is on the site and as far as we can tell, it looks up to the task of digging the foundation. All we need now is for the weather pattern to shift so that it rains on weekends and is clear during the week. Construction guys here do not work weekends. There's that work ethic thing again.

Thanks to those of you who have suggested I put these letters into a book at some future time. I'd have to be very selective about the material if I do that. I've just recently learned that Jesus loves me, so I don't want to risk alienation of our neighbors now that we're "in tight."

Peace and Love,
Leslie and Hope

July 17, 2005

Dear Friends,

We send greetings from the soggy holler. We've had a wet period, thanks to the remnants of Hurricane Dennis. It's rained at some point every day for the past six or seven. The saving grace in the mountains is that it can be raining in one spot and dry only a few hundred yards away. When it was pouring at our rental house it was dry as a bone at Happy Hollow and the crew was able to continue digging our foundation.

We've had a bit more time to explore this town of twelve hundred where we are renting a house. It's too bad we can't get married here because there's a bridal registry at the local hardware store. No kidding. Every local bride should be well equipped with the proper tools to deal with any situation, thanks to the registry. We wonder if it was a coincidence that directly below the sign for the bridal registry there was a display of axes.

We continue to be amazed at the array of free and inexpensive entertainment here, and I'm not talking about the supermarket. There are free concerts all over the area. All you have to do is bring something to sit on. As you would expect in this heart of Bluegrass Country, the ringing banjos and smoking fiddles get our feet tapping and our blood pumping. If we knew how to clog, we'd be up dancing with our neighbors.

We've heard that until fairly recently there was not much television in these mountains. Cable is very limited and satellite service was just not here. Many of the mountain people played instruments for their own entertainment, and they started playing at very young ages. The culture and tradition have nurtured an enormous wealth of musical talent.

Speaking of bluegrass music, we spent a wonderful day yesterday at the Alleghany County Fiddler's Convention. Our friend Joan is visiting from Atlanta and the three of us enjoyed some of the best music we've heard in the mountains. For $7 we got to spend the entire day listening to the various competitors for cash prizes. There was one kid about eight- or nine-years old, who was obviously some sort of musical prodigy. His guitar, mandolin and banjo playing were fantastic. I resolved to come home and burn my banjo after listening to him. Instead, we tried to overdose on junky festival food and had a grand time.

Not every aspect of country living is relaxing, though. We sat up late Friday night talking with Joan and then headed for bed. No sooner had we settled in than we heard some kind of racket coming from the attic. In this area an attic is referred to as a bonus room but no one told us we had an even bigger bonus—free pets! Most of our things are stored up there so you can imagine our frustration when we discovered an extended family of mice in residence.

We had installed one of those sound devices that are supposed to keep rodents away and set traps that netted a couple of victims a few weeks ago. We thought we had the problem under control but found out Friday night we were mistaken.

The noise was so loud it sounded like someone dragging furniture around. We finally decided that something was partially trapped and was trying to free itself. Surely, we reasoned, all of that noise could not be coming from a small mouse. Thinking it was a squirrel, raccoon or some larger animal, we hesitated to go up there. What would we do if it panicked and bit us? I spent the better part of an hour convincing Hope that it was not safe for her to go up there to investigate. She's the brave one when it comes to dealing with animals; I specialize in difficult humans.

By 2 a.m. it was impossible to sleep so I called the police. I asked if they could get someone from the animal control department to come out to see what was going on in our attic. We never heard back from them and I'm sure that's because they all died laughing at us. The officer was very polite but I suspect the minute he put the phone down, they had a good laugh at our expense.

The creature must have exhausted itself because it got quiet for awhile and we were able to get a few hours sleep. When daylight broke, Hope and I went upstairs and discovered not one, but two mice, each partially trapped in mousetraps. One was clearly alive, staring out at us from between two paintings, and the other was in a sorry state, barely alive and trying to hide in the insulation material. Luckily, Hope was not afraid to pick them up in a towel and take them outside.

I was very impressed with her bedside manner. She talked softly to them, calming them so she could scoop them up and take them out. Once outside, one scampered away (to return to the attic, I'm sure) and the other looked like it wasn't going to make it when she freed it from the trap.

There's a happy ending to the mouse story, at least for the mice. When we got home from the fiddler's convention last night, the weakened mouse was no longer in the towel on the ground where we left it. Joan suspected something ate it, but since we saw no signs of a struggle, we believe it recovered enough to get away. We've resolved not to put any more traps in the attic.

> Peace and Love,
> Leslie and Hope

July 25, 2005

Dear Friends,

The holler is ablaze with wildflowers and we're trying, mostly without success, to identify them. What we see is never exactly like what's in the books. It's those little subtleties that always prove problematic.

You have to be good at picking up subtle cues in other things here too. It's taken us at least ten trips to the dump to figure out that socializing ranks right up there with dumping trash. People do discard their trash after sorting it into about eight different categories, and then some of them just hang out, talking with one another over the back of a pickup truck...or in a pinch the trunk of a car will do.

We've been too intent on figuring out why they sort glass into only two categories, white and green. We've yet to figure out what to do with brown glass. We've been throwing it in with the green glass, waiting for the recycling police to show up at our door at any moment.

Using our cars for trips to the dump presents another challenge. It really hit home when I went from the dump to the grocery store and started to load the groceries into the trunk that had held our trash a mere thirty minutes earlier. Hope says I shouldn't worry about it, because the trash is always in closed plastic bags, but I still don't like the thought of mingling items representing the beginning and end of our food chain.

The dump isn't the only place people talk here. They chat wherever they are. The other day I was loading groceries into the car and I heard a voice say, "Sure is hot today." I looked around and saw a woman seated in a truck parked next to me. "Sure is," I replied. "Smighty good for growin' though," she continued. "I guess you're right about that," I answered. (Like I know anything about growing things)

She probably would have continued for a while, had I not gotten into my car and closed the door. I could see she was still saying something to me so I lowered the window. "Have a nice day," she said and smiled. I returned the sentiment and started to drive away. As I looked in my rear view mirror, I noticed she was waving goodbye.

Driving off, I tried to imagine where she came from and what her life was like. Was she lonely and taking full advantage of this opportunity to get out and socialize? She was using portable oxygen, and I guessed the person who drove her there was doing her grocery shopping, since she could not. Maybe next time I'll stay longer and talk more about the weather. After all, I'm retired now and don't have to be in a hurry. And so what if my frozen food melts.

One place where the food only melts in our mouths is Sweet Aromas, a wonderful local bakery and cafe. For us, it's the heart and soul of nearby West Jefferson. Paula, the proprietor, cook and general do-everything person, always greets us with a big hug and when time allows, stops by our table to visit. One of the favorite menu items is the world's best cinnamon buns. They are definitely worth abandoning any diet for, and we do so frequently.

During the recent Christmas in July event, Hope lent Paula a hand busing tables and peeling potatoes for a couple of hours. It lasted long enough for her to decide that was not a viable career option.

From our front porch the other morning, we watched a group of Latino workers in the Christmas tree field wielding their machetes as they cut vines and other unwelcome plants off the trees. It took considerable self-discipline to be able to calmly watch men with machetes heading in our direction, and refrain from calling the police and locking the doors. We did manage to remain calm and all is well—so far.

We want to thank all of you for your mice-chasing suggestions, but so far we have not resolved to get either snakes or cats.

Peace and Love,
Leslie and Hope

Dear Friends,

We enjoyed a four-day visit from Joanne, another of my old Newark friends, this week. It gave us yet another opportunity to show off the attributes of The High Country, as this area is known. We took in a free old-time music concert in a tiny town called Todd, not far from here. We heard a local band, The Corklickers, and relaxed on folding chairs with about a hundred other people. Every now and then, a man sitting near us would take out a piece of plywood and get up and dance on it in very fancy red and white clogging shoes. It was the smallest dance floor we'd ever seen, measuring about three by five feet.

We are amazed at the vitality of people in their seventies and eighties who do this clogging. I actually saw a woman I'd guess was in her late seventies in a wheelchair get up and clog and then return to her wheelchair without panting. I know they say if you do it all your life, it doesn't bother you, but I know I cannot jitterbug any longer without getting out of breath, and I was pretty young when I learned to do that. Of course, I got used to a sedentary lifestyle in the city and the people here are still very much used to hard physical work.

Hope's job search continues with a bit more promise. She's getting some positive signs from the university for a part-time, temporary job. She's been told by lots of places that she's way over-qualified, and we don't doubt that for a moment, but she still would rather be employed than be a woman of forced leisure.

I, on the other hand, am adapting nicely to my new life of leisure. The recent heat encouraged a few afternoon naps and I'm getting reacquainted with my banjo. I actually took it out on the porch to play the other day and didn't notice any wildlife fleeing.

We have just concluded our search for a four-wheel drive vehicle to replace Hope's Camry. Everyone tells us we'll need one here for the winter. You would not believe how they sell cars here! We spent all day Friday visiting dealers and test driving cars.

Our first stop was at a Subaru dealer, the one that operates on banker's hours. We managed to find it open this time and talked briefly with a salesman before asking to test drive an Outback. He went to get the keys, came back in a minute and told us to take our time with the test drive.

I was so stunned I could barely drive the car. No request for a license, fingerprints or anything. He had our nine-year old car there, but that would have made a lousy trade for him if we'd decided to skip town with the new Subaru. We guess they assume if you drive in, you have a driver's license and you're not a car thief.

The salesman was pleasant when we returned half an hour later, and said we planned to continue shopping around. No pressure selling. He barely seemed interested in selling the car at all. In fact, I had to ask for his card.

We had predetermined to test drive cars up to the top of Howard's Knob, a mountain that overlooks Boone. It's a very steep drive, one we'd never attempt in winter with any snow or ice. I did the first run up the mountain and as we neared the top, we smelled a strong burning odor. We were sure we'd burned up the engine and figured we'd probably burn up the brakes on the drive down. It's so steep that it's impossible not to ride the brake. Why anyone would want to live up there is beyond us.

When we returned the car, and told the salesman about the burning odor, he assured us it was a protective coating on the engine that we smelled, and that we'd done no harm. We were much relieved. We liked the car, but didn't want to have to buy it with a burnt-out engine.

The story for the rest of the day was much the same. No pressure tactics and they trusted us to take other cars out with no questions asked.

Hope got scared when we climbed into a five-speed manual transmission SUV in West Jefferson because she didn't think I'd remember how to drive it. We took a short ride but I chickened out when it came to climbing a mountain with a stick shift. After twenty years, could I keep it from sliding down the mountain backwards? If not, I could have wiped out Wal-Mart, the county high school, the civic center and a few other shops at the base of the mountain. Not a very neighborly gesture.

We ended up buying a Honda CR-V and to my great disappointment and Hope's equally great relief, it didn't come in taxi cab yellow. We had to settle for a sand color. I'm now insisting that I get to paint our garage bright yellow, hoping that it will reflect off the car and make the car look yellow. Hope is so relieved about the car color, that I think I can win this concession without too much of a struggle.

The footers on the new house are complete. We couldn't resist the temptation to carve our names and the date in the fresh cement. Unlike the last time I did that, I didn't get a whipping and nobody grounded me.

We've been enjoying the magical mountain views from our rental house. It kind of reminds me of those Magic Slate toys we played with as kids. Remember those tablets that you could draw on, and then lift the sheet of plastic and your drawing would disappear? Well, our magical mountain appears and disappears just like that. One minute you gaze out the window and see it in all its majesty, and then a few minutes later you look out and wonder if you were hallucinating because it's gone, hidden behind a wall of mist. 'Just another one of those simple pleasures in the holler. We miss all of you and hope to hear from you soon.

Peace and Love,
Leslie and Hope

August 7, 2005

Dear Friends,

The really big news from the holler is that the number of unemployed persons in this part of NC has decreased by three-fourths. Hope got a contract to teach a graduate course and work part time at the university. We are elated and hope this provides a foot in the door for a permanent position with benefits. The only benefit she gets with this is a discounted faculty parking permit. We celebrated with champagne, courtesy of our contractor, Nicole.

Do you recall the splash we made when we registered to vote in the holler? That was nearly seven weeks ago, and we still don't have our voter registration cards. When we called the Board of Elections and asked when we might expect them, the clerk told us, "There's nothin' to vote for comin' up soon." I guess that was her way of telling us to chill. When we pressed to find out what the hold-up was, we learned that our street isn't in the county computer. "Well," we asked. "What has to happen for it to get into the computer?" "I guess I can put it in now," was the answer. We were relieved to know this, because Hope nearly had me convinced that they "lost" our forms because they don't like our party affiliation.

I don't know if I mentioned that here in the Tarheel State they only require a rear license plate, or "tag," as the locals call it. That leaves you free to choose just about anything to put on the front of the car. There are some "official" front plates you can purchase at the tag office, and you wouldn't believe some of them.

How does, "I Love My Church" grab you? The ones sanctioned by the state carry the tag line, "First in Flight" referring to the Wright Brothers' flight at Kitty Hawk. Somehow that tag line just doesn't seem to go well with some of the plates. The other day I nearly died laughing when I saw one in a parking lot that said, "First in Flight" and beneath it in very large letters, "JESUS." Southwest Airlines look out!

We're thrilled to see the foundation of our house nearing completion. It's really starting to look like a house. I'll send a photo, and lest you suspect your eyes are playing tricks, I'll warn you that what you're looking at is indeed Styrofoam. It's the best insulation for a dry basement. They'll pour concrete into these forms, and then start working on the sub floor. If you've ever wondered what $45,000 worth of Styrofoam looks like, this will provide your answer.

We love hearing from you so keep those emails coming.

Peace and Love,
Leslie and Hope

August 14, 2006

Dear Friends,

The saga of our voter registration cards continues. We were supposed to receive our cards last Saturday, since they print cards on Fridays. Saturday came and went with no cards in sight. By Wednesday, we decided to pay a visit to the Board of Elections to see if some sinister plot was afoot. Feet play a major role in this, as we were to discover.

We were ushered into Billy Bob's office; he's the guy in charge of elections. I immediately noticed three empty shoes under his desk, not a good sign, I reasoned. Either he had three feet or perhaps no feet, since he didn't stand up to greet us.

We had a discussion about when we should expect to receive the cards in the mail, and discovered that the mail sometimes isn't picked up from the county offices on Saturday, "because nobody's there," according to Billy Bob. Good reason, I think. So, the wind up of this is that we might or might not get our cards next week, but I'm reminded of what the clerk told us earlier. There's nothing to vote for coming up anyway, so we'll just sit tight.

The question of whether or not Billy Bob has feet was resolved, by the way. He stood up to shake my hand, and when I reached across his desk, I saw his feet. No socks, and no shoes, but I did see feet. I also noticed four more shoes behind his desk. So the mystery of the odd number of shoes remains just that, a mystery. If I ever learn the explanation, I'll be sure to share it since I'm sure you're just dying of curiosity.

Another part of our settling-in process here in the holler involves finding all new doctors. I went to see my new internist this week and was the youngest patient in the waiting room, by far. I was also the warmest.

When I walked into the office, it was at least ten degrees colder in there than it was outside, and it was in the 70's outside. It was freezing in there, and I was dressed in a T-shirt and jeans, my dress-up outfit since retiring to the holler. I looked around for a seat in a warmer part of the room, and picked one.

Two of the elderly ladies told me not to sit there or I'd freeze to death. They obviously had scoped out the whole waiting room. They directed me to a warmer seat, but after two minutes I went to the car for my long-sleeved denim shirt. When I came back in with it, one of the ladies asked if she could share it. Being friendly now in the way of the holler, I told her, "Come sit by me and I'll give you a sleeve."

I've never seen a group of people in a doctor's waiting room get into a conversation before. Usually people just read, or they're too sick to want to talk. Within a minute, we were all discussing the temperature, and one lady said we should all refuse to take off our clothes if the examining room was equally cold. Everyone agreed, and just then the nurse came to call the next patient. She called out, "Snow" and before I could censor myself, I asked, "Is that a weather forecast for this office?" The ladies thought that was hilarious and Mrs. Snow got up to go inside. The nurse was not amused. Before we could get anything going with the protest movement, I was called in, and grateful to discover that it wasn't as cold in the examining room.

By the way, the doctor actually spent half an hour with me, listened to my answers to his questions, and was not typing on a laptop while we talked. That was a pleasant change. Now, before you go and assume that we don't have laptops here let me assure you that technology in the holler is very much alive and well. The only difference I've detected is that it's a bit slower, like everything else, and that computers and email have not yet replaced good old face-to-face conversation.

That's enough of this conversation. Take care.

Peace and Love,
Leslie and Hope

August 21, 2005

Dear Friends,

We discovered a hollerism that we cannot figure out. Maybe one of you knows what a koozie is. We were at a bluegrass event last weekend and they handed out door prizes. One of them contained four koozies, and we're curious to know what they are. We didn't want to act like foreigners and show our ignorance by asking people around us, so we just acted like we hear about koozies all the time, and applauded the winner. The winner wasn't sitting anywhere near us, so we couldn't sneak a peek at them.

Life is pretty idyllic, but even here in the holler there are occasional things that aggravate us. Nearly every day we pass a motel on our way into town with one of those signboards that includes messages of all sorts. For weeks now it's been irritating to see the congratulations messages spelled "congradulate." We've resisted the temptation to go in and tell them how to spell it, but it's really annoying. After all, we don't want tourists to think we're all illiterate here.

Perhaps it was coincidental, but the other day, the very same day the schools reopened, someone corrected the spelling. We're not sure what happened after months of lousy spelling, but we're speculating that once school opened, some underpaid teacher took a job as night clerk at the motel, and corrected the message. We feel much better. All we need to do now is find out what "Git er done." with two people's names beneath it means. That often appears on the signboard too.

I'm thrilled to be able to conclude the saga of the voter registration cards. I received not one, but four voter cards today. This is beginning to sound like my native New Jersey, where people vote early and often in some places. You won't believe the location of our polling place. It's called "big fields." If we start looking now, by the time there's anything to vote for, we might locate the big fields. Maybe we'll just ask the cows; they should be able to tell us.

I know you will find this nearly impossible to believe, but in just two short months, the status that eluded me for more than sixty years in the North, has finally been achieved here in the holler. I have managed to become a southern lady. How do I know this? I learned it in a gas station the other day.

With gas prices varying from one station to another, I naturally sought out the place with the cheapest gas, and started to put the nozzle into my gas tank. The attendant came running over and said he'd do that. I said that I didn't realize it was a full-service station, and he informed me that, "It is for ladies and some elderly gentlemen." I didn't ask what constituted "elderly" or I would surely have had to forget my newly-conferred status as a lady and deck him.

If you're guessing what my response was, I'll bet you're wrong. I smiled sweetly and said, "Isn't that nice?" Now, before you start wondering if I've completely abandoned my feminist principles since moving to the holler, let me tell you that we southern ladies say, "Isn't that nice?" as a substitute for "Go ----- yourself." It's just so much more genteel to smile and say, "Isn't that nice?" and leave the person wondering what you really meant. This guy didn't have a clue, I'm sure.

This whole thing contrasts with the fact that our area is represented in the U.S. Senate and House of Representatives by two very strong women. No one has ever accused Elizabeth Dole of needing assistance, I'm sure, and our Congresswoman is mean as a snake and tough as nails.

I prefer to look at this chauvinism in a very pragmatic way. When we're in the dead of winter and I don't want to freeze my behind off by getting out of the nice warm car to fill the gas tank, I will surely rejoice in my newfound status, and let some guy do it. After all, I must demand equal treatment with elderly gentlemen.

We miss all of you and wish you were here.

Peace and Love,
Leslie and Hope

August 28, 2006

Dear Friends,

For those of you who venture to the holler, you'll feel right at home. The first thing you'll notice is that the grand homogenization of America has not bypassed us. Driving into West Jefferson you'll see Arby's, Taco Bell, KFC and the ubiquitous McDonald's. Perhaps they're featuring some regional specialties like deep fried possum burgers, or rattlesnake nuggets. We haven't investigated yet.

We've already discovered one local delicacy that we can live without. It took us awhile to figure out what that elongated thing was on Hope's plate the other day. From its shape, it could have been many things, none of which we wanted any part of, but Hope bravely tried it and pronounced it a deep fried pickle. If you grew up as we did on kosher deli pickles, we can't recommend it. There are just some things that in the name of decency shouldn't be done to pickles.

I've already talked about how friendly people in the holler are, and there are so many different styles of greeting that we've been wondering if our responses are appropriate. We wouldn't want people to think we're unfriendly or weird. We've already mastered "Hey" instead of "Hi," and now know when to use the finger greeting when driving, but we're still not sure how we're supposed to respond when a man nods at us. Only men nod; women usually smile and speak. We've tried to watch other women to see how it's done, but everybody here knows one another, so folks stop and chat. That doesn't help us much.

I finally got up the nerve to ask someone about it. I decided to ask Eric, our flamboyant holler florist who has lived here all of his life. Don't let the flamboyant descriptor throw you; he's got a wife and four kids. Whether or not they're window dressing, we don't know.

Eric plays show tunes in his shop and has confided to me that his great ambition is arranging flowers for New York theaters so he can see plays, preferably musicals. He thinks I'm quite worldly, since I lived near New York for many years and actually saw plays on Broadway.

I told Eric about my dilemma, not knowing what the correct response is when a man nods at me. If I smile, I'm afraid I'll seem like I'm being too forward, since he doesn't smile. He just nods. Eric says I should just nod. He said this advice would hold true for hat tippers too. So, now I know another form of greeting. One must be proper about these things.

My next task is to discover why Eric calls me "Miss Leslie," and just calls Hope by her name. I think I know the answer, and it has something to do with my gray hair, but I'll wait awhile until I know him better before I question this custom. So far, he's the only one who does that.

As a city person, I've always been fascinated by farm animals. I think I can learn a lot from observing the cows near our house. They really know how to relax, and I found out this week, they also know how to party.

I had always heard there are gay animals, but had never seen any. That is, until this week, when we learned there are definitely lesbian cows. We observed irrefutable evidence that there are at least two in the herd down the road from our house. We'll keep an eye on this situation, and see if we can add to the body of scientific evidence that this is a naturally occurring phenomenon. I wish I could have read the mind of the bull in the adjacent pasture as he witnessed the two of them, udders flapping, having a gay old time.

There's a famous local painting called "The Hanging of Will Banks" that we saw in the lawyer's office, as we were signing our wills the other day. It turns out that Will was hanged publicly right here in Ashe County for shooting his uncle over an argument that had to do with fifty cents. We're told the onlookers in the painting are recognizable forbears of our holler neighbors, just out for a Sunday picnic and hangin'. 'Guess we got here too late for the event. It happened in the early 1900's. It was the last public hanging in North Carolina, thank goodness.

Speaking of shooting, I want you all to know that a special edition of a Luger 44-millimeter pistol is being produced with engravings of the Ashe County Courthouse and other scenes from the county, in fourteen-carat gold and silver plate. This is a limited edition, so hurry and put your order in if you want one. They're a bargain at $450. Remember, though, that you can't carry a concealed weapon into the library here, so you'd better get a see-through holster for it. What a nice idea for Christmas or Hanukkah.

On that note, we'll sign off.

Peace and Love,
Leslie and Hope

August 31, 2005

Dear Friends,

I learned this morning that we missed a major geological event yesterday. There was an earthquake in western North Carolina, a wee one by geological standards, but one that people said they felt. We were too busy running around with our visiting friends to notice, but I can't help wondering if it occurred while we were sitting in a Boone restaurant having lunch, and I announced I was going to buy an oil portrait of George Bush that was on display. Of course I wasn't serious, but I wonder if the gods in the cosmos realized that.

A note about house progress is in order. They finished the basement as of Monday. I watched as they poured the contents of eight cement trucks into the foundation walls. It was fascinating, and I delighted in the knowledge that at least we were doing our part in staking a claim to a substantial amount of concrete for the good old USA. Despite their wild construction boom, the Chinese weren't getting this concrete!

Hope started the job at the university and began her adjunct teaching this week. She had the dubious advantage of having four former teachers offer her advice on how she should teach her course. All of our visiting friends taught for several years, and naturally, I had to add my two-cents too. We sat up until 2 a.m. discussing the lesson until we all were ready to drop in our tracks. I'm sure she was tickled to get back to work the next day to plan her first lesson without our help. Despite all of the unsolicited advice, the class met Thursday night and all went well.

Those of you who know and love Hope can appreciate that she still thinks graduate students should work hard and earn their credits. No amount of persuasion could convince her that they just want to get the credits, and that she shouldn't expect them to embrace a rigorous course. She still thinks grad students want to learn. Imagine that! I can hardly wait until reality sets in, as she tracks their progress. It shouldn't be too long before the first student complains that he should have gotten a higher grade because he showed up for all classes.

Speaking of tracking things, we've always wondered where the four-legged wildlife was at Happy Hollow. Until now, all we'd seen were some wild turkeys. I finally spotted a mother deer and her fawn, and most interesting of all, learned that a neighbor saw a black bear on our property a few weeks ago. I hope it didn't dine on our Styrofoam foundation material, or we'll be finding a really cranky, constipated bear in the not-too-distant future.

It's one thing for us to become familiar with local customs, but now we are moving a step beyond that. We're learning to speak "You all" with the help of a book Hope received recently. In the vernacular of our new home, we are about to leave "barefoot season" and enter "chestnut time." I just love the visual imagery of southern speech.

The southerners manage to describe things in a way that instantly activates your mind's eye. I love this one. "He couldn't organize a piss-off in a brewery." Sometimes, though, my imagination fails me. I'm still trying to figure out how "Don't strain your egg bag," means you shouldn't try to kid me. Some just make me laugh trying to picture them. A favorite is "A closed mouth gathers no foot."

We are enjoying a precursor to chestnut time this week. Color is starting to appear on the trees and shrubs and there's a definite chill in the morning air. We're approaching quilt-sleeping time in the mountains.

When you find your way to the holler, we must take you to the Mast Store, an old-fashioned general store that sells gadgets that remind me of my childhood back in ancient times. The best thing is an assortment of what used to be called "penny candy." They have Walnettos, Mary Janes and dozens of other items guaranteed to yank out your fillings and crowns.

I had an inspiring thought while browsing in there last week. I could make a fortune marketing dental services by inserting a small card in each candy bag advertising a 10% discount on dental work. I haven't yet figured out how to get dentists to offer discounts, though. That's in my retirement projects file.

Well friends, it's time to close and I can't think of a better way than to offer this bit of advice from the holler. Live one day at a time and scratch where it itches.

Peace and Love,
Leslie and Hope

- 2 -

Soaking up Local Color

September 4, 2005

Dear Friends,

It's getting quieter in the holler these days and even more so in the evenings. The tourist population in the mountains is shrinking, as people either make peace with their home environments, or stay here and go kicking and screaming into fall. We attribute the very quiet nights to two things; the high price of gas that causes people to stay off the roads, and the tree toads have stopped doing whatever it is they do to cause that nighttime noise.

We tend to keep the TV and music off so we can read or look at paint chips. Ah yes, we have reached the point in our home construction when we must make decisions about colors. Until now, we have faced little difficulty reaching agreement about the house. We agreed on the design, style of logs and the kind of foundation quite easily. We even agreed on the choice of lighting and bathroom fixtures without a struggle. But we have met our Waterloo, and it's located in the Benjamin Moore and Sherwin-Williams paint stores. We are engaged in what Hope calls the "color wars."

These so-called discussions are reminiscent of the Christmas tree debates before we bought an artificial tree many years ago.

Without naming names, let us just say that one of us feels no need to look at every color in the universe when she finds one she really likes. The other one insists on looking at every color in the known world, even after she sees what she likes.

The Christmas tree thing was easy to resolve; one of us sat in the warm car while the other froze her behind off and looked at every tree in the forest. This color situation has eluded resolution so far. If there really is such a thing as "intelligent design" I can't think of a better time for it to present itself!

I'm amazed to find that people here genuinely enjoy very simple pleasures. The other day I was having some blood work done, and the technician asked what I did. When I told her I was retired, I got the usual response that she wished she were also. Then she continued, telling me what she wants to do when she retires—cook, clean her closets and basement and paint her house. I just smiled, winced really. She was sticking a needle in my arm. I thought to myself that if I'd been promised I'd be doing those things when I retired, I'd still be working.

For the past couple of weeks I've been immersing myself in local history. This is quite an interesting area. I learned, for instance, the reason this area is so heavily Republican is that during the Civil War many of the residents were pro-Union, and as a result supported Lincoln's Republican Party. I think it's time they figured out that George W. Bush is no Abe Lincoln; they need to get over it.

I've discovered that the holler has its own radio station. It's the only station that has very local information about what's happening, so I try to listen to it in the morning. I say "try," because depending on the time, if I don't hit it right, I can end up with a mini-sermon and the hymn hour.

The other morning I was amused to note that the program host spent more time apologizing for a national news feed that included the New Orleans mayor expressing frustration with the federal government's lousy response to Hurricane Katrina, than he did reading the news. The mayor used the term "Goddamn" in an interview and the local announcer said the station would file a formal request to the Associated Press to please edit (read that as censor) such "crude, vulgar language" from the news, before sending it to us sheltered folk in the mountains. Imagine what the mayor would have to say if he heard that!

The horrible effects of the hurricane on the Gulf coast have inspired our community to throw itself into charitable efforts. They're on a rather small scale compared to what we were used to outside the holler, but these are people who can't afford much. Proportionately, I'm sure they are doing more than many people who are far more affluent.

One woman actually cried on the radio when she described the reaction of a woman in Mississippi who found out that two trailer truckloads of water were being sent from this small town in Appalachia. These are good people who really feel for others in need.

They are collecting food and sundries in supermarket parking lots and trying to raise the money to put gas in the trucks for the drive to the Gulf area. I'd love to hear of some local gas stations donating gas, but they're behaving like gas stations all across the country; they're gouging.

I'm learning about the local people's views of the summer influx of Floridians. Several have second homes here, where they spend the hottest months of the year. While the infusion of capital to the local economy is appreciated, I'm sure, people here seem to get weary of Floridians trying to change the way things are done in the holler. I love one bumper sticker I see on pickup trucks. It reads, "We don't care HOW you do it in Florida."

I'm glad we're not from Florida. I used to think it was bad enough telling folks we're from up north, but that's not quite as bad as being from Florida. But then, most of the Floridians I've met are really transplanted New Yorkers, so maybe it is a Yankee thing after all. I can always tell people I'm half-southern by blood; my father's family was from Richmond, Va. I'll save that piece of ammunition in case I get into a tight situation.

Stay in touch. We miss all of you.

Peace and Love,
Leslie and Hope

September 8, 2005

Dear Friends,

We're doing well and finding it hard to believe we've been in the holler for three months. In many ways it seems like longer; we feel so comfortable here. Every time I have to ask someone to repeat what they've said, though, I'm reminded that we are still foreigners here. I always expect people to have trouble understanding us, but it hasn't happened—or maybe they're just too polite to say so.

I was in the local carpet store the other day, deeply immersed in Berbers, when a man entered the store and said "Good morning." I smiled and returned the greeting and he told me I added an element of "gorgeousness" to the merchandise and that I should spend more time there. I smiled again, thanked him, and returned to the Berber samples.

A few minutes later he was back, asking me if I knew how radiant my smile was. I started to get a bit suspicious, but remained friendly since the owner was right near me. He left shortly after that and just as I was feeling pretty puffed up by his compliments the owner quickly put a damper on my inflated ego. She told me not to pay him any attention because he's "not well."

We try to take in as many cultural events as we can, so when we learned about a Bar-B-Q cook-off, we made plans to go with friends Mack and Ted. We were driving around with them, trying to find the event from the description in the newspaper, and having difficulty locating it. Finally, in desperation, we stopped and Mack called out to a man walking by for some directions. As we pulled away, Mack insisted that it be noted for the record that he was a man asking for directions, but Ted just as quickly said that it doesn't count, because he's gay. We still take that to be a promising sign. Incidentally, the event had been cancelled, and no one bothered to announce it.

I've been spending more time listening to our local radio station. I find I'm learning lots about holler life that way. Maybe this is done in lots of small towns, but I've never heard of a radio station reading the obituaries from each funeral home. It starts to sound like readings from the *Old Testament* after awhile. The announcer not only tells you the name of the deceased; he lists all the begats and grand- and great-begats as well. They all seem to end with the phrase, "and several nieces and nephews also survive."

Fear not. Equal time is given to naming all of the newborns at the local hospital too. If this week is any indication, the Latino population will soon become the dominant group here. Out of five babies announced this week, only one had a non-Latino surname. It seems odd to hear those names in Appalachia, but the Christmas tree industry attracts migrants from Mexico and other Central American countries, and unlike the past, when they were just seasonal workers, now they are becoming residents. Amen to that. We're starting to see some great restaurants opening here.

More house progress this week. Our basement is nearly finished, the septic tank is in, and the well has been tested for radon. Don't I sound "country?"

There is peace in the holler, or at least a truce. The color wars appear to have ended in our home. We've finally decided on colors for the sheetrock walls, and flooring for the rooms that will be carpeted. I have spent enough time in the carpet store to qualify for a license in interior decorating, or at the very least, adoption by the owners. Come to think of it, the latter is probably preferable because I know I never, ever want to do all this shopping again.

You will undoubtedly be as thrilled as we are to know that a new chapter of The John Birch Society is forming in the holler. 'Remember them from the 60's? Their mission now is to "protect" the Constitution, and they're scheduling meetings to educate the public about the Constitution. For about thirty-seconds I toyed with the idea of going to one of the meetings, but wisdom prevailed and I realized it would not be a good thing. The likelihood of my being able to keep my mouth shut when they give out misinformation is about zero, or less. I reminded myself that I'm determined to stay relaxed, and that would not contribute to my new state of calm.

We took a trip to Winston-Salem, the closest major city, to stock up on some supplies at Costco. It was Hope's first trip "down mountain" as they say here, and only my second. Once we were in Winston, as it's called, we were immediately reminded of why we left an urban environment. Everyone was in a big hurry, and people leaned on their horns the minute the traffic light turned green. That's not done in the holler.

No one there called me Ma'am or even said "Have a nice day." And we quickly remembered we should not greet strangers or smile at them. Oh well, what can you expect from a city named for two kinds of cigarettes? After an hour down there I was more than ready to return to the holler. It's funny how quickly we've come to appreciate the increased level of civility and the slower pace of life here.

On that calm note, we'll wish y'all a good week.

Peace and Love,
Leslie and Hope

September 18, 2005

Dear Friends,

We're still enjoying spectacular weather here in the holler. Days are in the mid- to upper-seventies with an occasional spike to the 80-degree mark. At night we're cozy with a quilt since it drops down into the upper 40's and 50's. I've gotten into the habit of having my breakfast in sweat pants and a fleece jacket until it warms up. We're trying to delay putting on the heat until we absolutely have to, since energy costs more here. We could claim to be conserving natural resources, but in truth we're really conserving monetary resources. Or, as they say in the holler, we're close chewers and tight spitters (frugal).

We've spotted the first load of Christmas trees heading for some foreign (outside NC) market. Neighbors tell us the traffic here is unbelievable when the out-of-towners arrive the day after Thanksgiving to choose and cut their own trees. We're nestled in among several tree farms so it should be interesting. I want to set up a hot toddy stand and make a few dollars while they're here but Hope is dead set against it since this is a dry county. Too bad I didn't think of this idea a few weeks ago; it could have been a bargaining chip in the color wars.

Some of you who've visited the holler have seen the herd of buffalo roaming in a nearby meadow. They're getting fuzzier now that the weather has cooled, and they really do look like those immense creatures that used to be found all over the central and western plains. They're a good reminder that we are not only southerners but westerners as well. We are, after all, living in the heart of Daniel Boone country. Little did I imagine when I rode the neighbor's fence in Newark and sang *Home on the Range*, I'd one day have a home where the buffalo roam. Yes, we also have deer, but no antelope that I know of.

Life in the High Country is quite idyllic but also has its challenges. I learned during a visit to the allergist that I am apparently reacting badly to mountain allergens. The fact that we keep the windows wide open probably doesn't help the situation.

I'll undergo tests soon to see what in particular is causing the problem but until, then I'll just keep talking through my nose and let the locals assume it's my Yankee accent. If my mother were alive I'm sure she'd tell me I'm being punished for all those bad jokes I made about mouth breathers. The good news about all of this is that we're now a two-snorer family. I'm getting even.

We had a couple of exciting events in town this week. People's Drug store had a sale on freshwater pearls. Of course, we resisted the temptation to buy them. They'd look pretty tacky with jeans.

The second item of note was the arrival of the Christian Wrestling Federation for a match. I'd never heard of this group but they're pretty popular here. I'm imagining the Christians lined up on one side of the ring and all of the sinful (fun) things in life lined up on the other side. When the referee rings the bell, we get to watch the Christians wrestle with their demons, as they try valiantly not to give in to the temptations we all enjoy so much. My money's on the Christians, at least in public.

Well, before I exhaust you with too much excitement, I'll sign off for now. Y'all come visit. We miss you.

Peace and Love,
Leslie and Hope

September 24, 2005

Dear Friends,

It's very tempting to ignore the rest of the world when you've living in an area like the holler. Some days we don't even read a newspaper or watch TV news. The other evening for example, we went to a neighbor's home for dinner and walked into their living room to find their TV tuned to the news. It occurred to us that we had not heard or seen anything of the outside world for more than twenty-four-hours. We hoped we weren't being attacked or about to be hit by a hurricane.

As a recovering news junkie I am assisted in kicking my addiction by the fact that it's hard to find newspapers here. Unless, that is, you have a pocketful of quarters. Almost no stores carry newspapers; they're all in boxes on the street or in parking lots.

For someone who used to read two or more newspapers every day because of my work, this detachment is pretty significant. For about the first two weeks in NC, I felt somewhat adrift without my daily dose of stress-inducing news, but now I welcome it. Some evenings I grudgingly put on *Jim Lehrer's News Hour* and immediately regret it.

I worry that my enjoyment of this detachment from the world might land me in the pages of some academic journal one day. Some sociologist might write about the holler and mention this woman who used to do public relations in the Washington, D.C. area back in the early 2000's, and now doesn't even know who the president is. Come to think of it, there are days now when I wish I didn't know that.

I do sneak a peek at the *Washington Post* or *New York Times* online from time to time, but please don't assume if anything major happens that we know about it. If it's big news, call and let us know. If it's negative, know that you can always escape to our mountains. We have plenty of room for you here.

I find the weeklies far more interesting than the dailies from Charlotte or Winston-Salem. For several years before we moved to the holler we read *The Mountain Times* online and we continue to look forward to its appearance on Thursdays. It's got strictly local news, and if you don't mind loose writing and editing, it's not bad. It's free and lists local entertainment, so we use it to fill our social calendar.

We also have *The Jefferson Post*, which publishes twice weekly. It's written better than the *Times* and also covers local news. If you add up the news in it, it's got about two pages worth, and the rest consists of church notices, obituaries, school lunch menus and advertisements. Once in awhile we spring for fifty cents to buy it.

As I said, you have to have quarters to get a newspaper. No quarters, no newspapers. The exception is the free *Mountain Times*. Sometimes when I read it I'm reminded of what my mother used to say. "You get what you pay for, or you get nothing for nothing." As proof of that, she used to love telling us that she met my father at a free dance.

On Sundays, when we want to get *The Charlotte Observer* we raid our quarter jar. The purpose of the jar has evolved. It used to be where we popped our quarters to save for trips down here. We got pretty good too. Sometimes we saved enough to pay for a couple of nights in a motel. Now, it's been downgraded to a depository for newspaper money. Like a lot of others things, it's been scaled down since I retired.

Progress on our house is really picking up speed. I was on site to see the first batch of logs arrive, and it was thrilling! The builder put up all the trusses, installed the sub- floor, framed the basement walls and began putting on the logs. It's so exciting to see it moving faster now.

Before you know it, we'll be in our new home. We can't wait.

Peace and Love,
Leslie and Hope

September 28, 2005

Dear Friends,

'Remember the Christian Wrestling Federation? I just couldn't believe my eyes when I glanced at the headline of the story about their match at the local high school. Are you ready for this? It read, "Pinned to the Mat by Christ." I couldn't have done better if I'd drunk a bottle of Scotch and started writing headlines, and you know I can't hold my liquor worth a damn. The same issue of the paper carried a story about the principal reporter for that paper who is going on a mission to convert Native Americans. Guess who wrote the headline and story about the wrestlers.

I might just have to write to the publisher one of these days. Perhaps I'll give my letter the header, "Up to the Eyeballs in Christ" or maybe "Christ up the Wazoo" would be catchier. I have nothing against Christianity, if you overlook the Crusades and the Inquisition, but this is getting to be too much.

On a more humorous note, I ran into my first holler huckster this week. I answered the door one day to find some guy who introduced himself as Cletus. After the obligatory conversation about the weather, he handed me his business card, shook my hand and said he needed me to do him a favor. In my best, most caring manner, I asked, "Whatcha need?" He proceeded to tell me he came all the way here from Bristol, Tenn. to deliver steaks, chicken and seafood to his regular customers, and they're not home. He "needed" me to buy the food, and promised he'd give me a great price.

The terms "avian flu" and "mad cow disease" kept flashing through my cynical brain. I gave him credit for an imaginative sales pitch but told him we're vegetarians. He looked puzzled. Maybe he thought that was a religion. He took back his card and headed up the road to ask the next family to do him a favor. While it has been a few months since I met a real live con artist, I am not so out of practice that I don't know bullshit when I see it. Give me another six months, though, and I might succumb.

We visited the mill where our logs were prepared and had a chance to see the various machines that size and shape the logs.

It's fascinating to watch, especially since we got to see some of our own logs being milled. Some were already wrapped and ready for shipment to our site. Our contractor doesn't deliver them all at once, in order to protect them from unnecessary exposure to the elements.

We continue to be impressed with the abundance of talent available here in the holler. Our cousin Lisa was visiting with us from New York this week and we took her to see "The Foreigner" performed by the local community theater group.

The subject matter was quite interesting for this area. It poked lots of fun at the mountain speech dialect, and also at the Klan. We were not quite sure how the rest of the audience took the latter part, but they all seemed to laugh when we did, a good sign. The actors were all local people and they did a great job. Lisa pronounced it a success and said it was better than some off-Broadway plays she'd seen. I guess you could say this is extremely off-Broadway, and well worth the $10 investment for a ticket.

We gave Lisa the full holler treatment this weekend. She got a personal tour of West Jefferson, including the famous murals, the bridal registry at True Value Hardware, the cheese factory, and our favorite restaurant, Sweet Aromas, home of the irresistible cinnamon buns. We wrapped up the tour with a meal at Woodlands Barbecue for authentic North Carolina BBQ, and wound up at Blowing Rock's most famous ice cream parlor. We're sending her home in a barrel.

We're getting pretty good at this southern hospitality thing. Come check us out.

Some of you have asked me about these updates, so let me assure you that what I put in them is all true. I know it sounds like fiction, but it's not. Who could possibly make up this stuff? Also, while Hope lends her name to them, she is guilty only by her association with me. I take full blame for the contents.

Peace and Love,
Leslie and Hope

October 2, 2005

Dear Friends,

This week definitely marked the change of seasons in the holler. We started it in T-shirts and ended up in jackets. We didn't quite hit a frost, but we came close with temperatures in the 30's one night. This should accelerate the exodus of the Floridians. We'll be curious to see if our Yankee blood can still handle the cold.

The level of personal service here still amazes us. For example, the other day I asked Paula of Sweet Aromas when she'll be serving my favorite, Three Sisters Soup. Her answer: "When do you want it?" I picked a day and sure enough, she had it on the menu. When's the last time you got to pick a menu item in a restaurant?

For those of you who thought I wasn't serious when I said we were living in the West, I wish you could have read the front page article in one of the local newspapers about thirty-nine year-old Gary Wyatt Earp (I'm not kidding; it's his real name.) who copped a guilty plea in the shooting death of his lover's estranged husband. He'll get out in five years, which tells you something about how that sort of thing is viewed by the law here. The article didn't say whether he is kin to the famous lawman, but I'm guessing he must be with a name like that.

Hope is a candidate for a couple of full-time academic jobs and has learned that even in academia, things are done differently here. It seems they contact references first and then decide whether to interview a candidate. They also ask references if they can provide the names of other people they can talk with about the candidate. We thought that was pretty weird, but a friend suggested the whole thing is probably being handled by Homeland Security these days. We all know how dangerous libraries can be, with all of those subversive books.

We two math-challenged people seem to have landed in the right place. Despite all of the bragging about the local schools, and the high scores students make on standardized tests, we've seen signs that we're not the only math-challenged people in the holler. We're trying to figure out how to approach the county parks commission to tell them the sign on the quarter-mile walking track that reads

.4 mile is wrong. They might be touchy about that.

One group of folks that has no problem with math, thank goodness, is our building crew. It's interesting to watch them measure things four and five times before they put a piece of wood on the house. I watched one guy send a piece of tongue and groove panel back to the cutter four times before it was exactly what he wanted for the underlayment of the roof.

I think I've resolved one issue that has been nagging at me since moving to the holler. People here think we Yankees talk fast. Compared to local residents we do, and I think I know why. They inject lots of extra syllables into words and that's why it takes them longer to say things. For example, that thing that sits in the living room and produces light is called a "lay-ump" here. A tiger is really "strip-ed." Get the picture?

Our friend Mary Ann's name has four syllables instead of the usual three. Her name is pronounced "Mary Ay-un" in these parts. I don't think we stand a snowball's chance in Hell of convincing them to drop those extra syllables, so I guess we'll have to learn their way. Or as we say, "When in Ro-um..."

There are a couple of notable exceptions to this pattern, of course. 'Just enough to confuse us. We are used to saying "you all" and they shorten the whole thing to "y'all." If we formalize it by saying, "all of you" they shorten that too; it becomes "all y'all." On balance, however, there are many more words with those extra syllables than ones with fewer, so speech is definitely slower here.

Do you remember the bridal registry I told you about? With Christmas approaching, the local radio station is announcing the names of couples who are registered at the True Value hardware store, and promoting it as a way of doing gift shopping. They claim to have some bridal consultants in the store to help people choose their dish patterns. When I was in there, all I saw was Corelle and other hard-to-break dishes along with some genuine Mason jars.

Until the next update, we hope you're keeping your powder dry and not talking too fast.

Peace and Love,
Leslie and Hope

October 9, 2005

Dear Friends,

We attended a performance of the North Carolina Symphony this week. The high school auditorium was filled with a very different audience than the ones we'd seen at the bluegrass concerts. Dress was much more formal. We even saw a couple of men in suits and ties. 'No overalls in sight at this concert.

We heard a work by a composer I'd never heard of, Sir William Walton. At first, when we saw the program listed in the newspaper, I thought he might be part of the family that included John Boy, Elizabeth, Jim Bob and Erin, but he's not. It was a grand evening at the unbelievable cost of—get this—$12 a ticket. The cultural offerings here are fewer than in the DC area, but at least we can afford to partake of them without breaking the bank.

Speaking of culture, I took advantage of a warm day and took my banjo out on the porch to play. I observed a phenomenon that I had also noted in Maryland. When I would play near an open window there, I'd see birds come and perch on a nearby limb. The same thing happened here. As soon as I started playing, they all seemed to swarm over to the area near the porch. No, they're not carrying picket signs or wearing earplugs. They really seem to like the music. There must be something about the vibrations that are pleasing to them. I stopped playing and they flew away. When I started again, they came back. I'll continue to give bird concerts as long as the weather permits. It's my small contribution to the ambience of the holler.

With Halloween approaching, we had some tricks in the holler this week. The first trick occurred with our heat. The landlord left us precise instructions about operating the appliances, but not a word about the heat. We tried it out for the first time and found it didn't work. At least, we thought it didn't.

This was another one of those embarrassing situations that probably gave some locals a chance to show how dumb Yankees are. It turns out the thing works just fine, if you know the trick. We didn't, but now we do, since the builder of the house came and showed us. The Two Stooges Construction Co.* can now add heating to its list of offerings.

Our greatest treat was a visit from dear friends Joanne and Deb from Maryland. We refined our first-time visitor itinerary and threw in a Halloween pot luck or "pitch-in" as one friend here calls it, with some new friends and future neighbors at Happy Hollow.

Just as I thought I was getting the hang of the western NC dialect, I ran into a challenge that took the wind out of my sails. I called to get an address and directions to a cabinetry shop down in Wilkesboro so Hope could go pick up some stain samples, and I literally could not even understand the man's name. It was really awkward when I finally got it and realized I'd met him at our house a mere two days before. His name is Ree-yuck or Rick, to those of you who don't speak Mountainese. Once we got that out of the way, I had to ask him to spell out the name of every road he mentioned as he gave me directions. I felt so bad that I actually told him I have a hearing problem (which I don't) so he wouldn't think it was his fault. That helped heaps. He turned the volume up and despite his shouting, I still couldn't understand him. We finally got through that agonizing conversation, and Hope did find her way to his shop.

We had very tricky weather this week. In one day we had sunshine, sleet, snow and temperatures ranging from thirty to fifty-two. With the thermometer reading thirty that morning, I put on my down parka with the hood buttoned under my chin and headed out for the supermarket. It's only two miles down the road, but when I got there and looked at the other people in the parking lot I thought I'd landed in a different climate zone. They were wearing sweatshirts or light denim jackets and no one had gloves or hats on, despite the sleet. When I opened the car door, I found out it was just as cold as when I'd left the house five minutes earlier. People looked at me strangely in my Nanook of the North outfit. I guess they don't take cold weather seriously here this early in the season.

One day, when a strong cold front was blowing through, I was working at the computer and saw something white fly by the window. With Halloween nearly here, I wondered if it was a Casper type of creature. It sure looked like some unearthly thing, though it was flying at Mach I speed, much faster than I think ghosts fly. It turned out to be a plastic bag from our trash can, the contents of which had been emptied by the wind. I spent the rest of the afternoon chasing our garbage cans around the neighborhood. This was not without reward, though. I stopped cursing just long enough to look up and see a beautiful rainbow over Mt. Jefferson. It's the first time I've seen a rainbow during a snow squall. Quite a treat!

We hope you're having more treats than tricks. Happy Halloween.

Peace and Love,
Leslie and Hope

* The Two Stooges Construction Co., a name we gave ourselves years ago because of our complete lack of talent for building or fixing anything.

October 16, 2005

Dear Friends,

One of the greatest bones of contention between my mother and me when I reached age fourteen had to do with my undying love of dungarees, as we called them in the fifties. The conflict came down to this. She thought it was time for me to outgrow my cowgirl phase, and I didn't. Mom always rejoiced when winter came and I had to put away my dungarees. I swapped denim for wool slacks, when I wasn't wearing school clothes. 'Remember school clothes? For those of you who are too young to remember, we used to wear different clothes to school from the grungy ones we wore for play.

Well, I think my dear mother must be rolling in her grave now, because I discovered fleece lined jeans this week. I marked a rite of passage by purchasing my first pair of Carhart jeans, a fixture in holler wardrobes. Happily, I can now maintain my retired look year round. The jean shopping experience was unique, to say the least.

After I told the saleswoman I wanted lined jeans, she asked me if I was having hot flashes! Depending on my answer, she said she'd steer me towards flannel or fleece linings. Actually, it made sense for her to try to determine my personal climate, but I was pretty surprised to be asked that question. Can't you just see a sales person in Bloomingdales or Macy's asking that? They'd probably be sued for infringing on someone's civil rights.

Some habits die hard, and the fall weather made me think of getting new shoes. After fifteen years of comfort, I decided I needed to replace my high-top, knock-around shoes. I tried to part with them in winters past, but every time I tried to find a replacement, I'd end up at the Dr. Scholl's counter for a new pair of gel sole cushions instead. After slipping on icy steps last week because the bottoms of those shoes are baby-ass smooth, I realized the time had come for the much-dreaded separation.

I went to every shoe store within twenty-five miles of the holler and learned that mountain women do not have narrow feet. I tried shoes on with thick socks to compensate for my skinny feet but there was just no fudging it; I can't wear anything but narrow width shoes, and they just don't sell them around here. I've had to order shoes online and hope they fit. If that doesn't work out, I'll have to go "down mountain." The big city has a greater diversity of everything, including shoe widths.

Imagine my frustration after spending a day looking for shoes with no luck. As some of you know, shopping isn't my favorite pastime in the first place. The topper to this aggravating day came when I retrieved our mail. One envelope jumped out at me. It was a mailing from one of the nearby Baptist churches and the message on the front read, "Don't let evolution make a monkey out of you." I couldn't resist opening it just to see how they planned to protect me from modern science, and saw an invitation to a creation conference on four successive Sunday nights this month. The agenda was tantalizing, and included such compelling questions as: Why do 75% of children raised in Christian homes lose their faith in the first year of college?; Are there lies in the textbooks?; Was there a global flood, and where did the water come from, and where did it go?; and my favorite topic, How dinosaurs are being used to brainwash our children. As further proof of their disdain for education, the invitation was from the Snake "Mountian" Baptist Church. 'Guess they don't approve of traditional spelling either. Too bad I'm busy and can't make it.

Tragedy came to the holler this week. As I approached Sweet Aromas to get my semi-monthly fix of Three Sisters Soup, my new mountain addiction, I was shocked by a sign on the door that said there would be no Moravian Chicken Pie until further notice. The sign said the reason was the chickens were on strike, and there would be no pie until their demands are met. Moravian pie is a specialty of the house, and I'm sure lots of folks were deeply disappointed. I saw this as an opportunity, however, and offered my services as a mediator. With my recent stint working for a union, I got used to dealing with unhappy workers, and thought I'd be pretty good at it, but they turned me down.

That's it from the holler for this week. Be well, stay warm and keep away from live chickens, especially if they're coughing and sneezing. That avian flu sounds horrible.

Peace and Love,
Leslie and Hope

October 23, 2005

Dear Friends,

For a few minutes, I thought I'd been dreaming that I was in the holler, and really had never left New Jersey. When I read the headline in the *Mountain Times*, "Big Brawl Coming," and they described a scene of people stamping their feet and clapping while watching fistfights, it sounded just like my old Newark high school at lunchtime. However, when I read on, it turns out this was a spectacle they actually expected people to buy tickets to observe. According to the organizer's promotion, "If you're man enough and have the guts, you're invited to enter and win the prize money, title, handsome trophy and bragging rights." In my high school we just fought to earn the right to keep our lunch money and our lives, and go to school another day. We didn't get trophies or prize money.

As I continue to learn about holler traditions, I just have to pass along this new knowledge, so you'll fit in when you come to visit. I just found out that Friday is "bean day" at the local drug store. How I missed that, I'll never know, but better late than never. The special on Fridays at the lunch counter is beans, cornbread and slaw (That's coleslaw for you Yankees.) I'm assuming that means pinto beans, a staple in the local diet. I'll have to go try it; I'm sure it'll be a gas.

I'm happy to report that at least one holler resident will not go barefoot this winter. UPS delivered my shoes and they fit. I don't know what people with skinny feet did before the Internet, but I'm grateful I can shop online. When I told one friend here about my shoe dilemma, this mountain woman said that women here are kept barefoot and pregnant, and that's why they have wide feet. Since she has no kids, I sure hope she was kidding.

Every night this week, they've been working at the tree farm, cutting and baling the trees, and loading them into refrigerated 18-wheeler trucks. Those must be the ones going pretty far. Others go in open trucks. When one of those passes by, we take a deep sniff to see if we can pick up the evergreen scent. The hillsides along the road leading to our house are changing from green to brown as they cut down the trees for shipping. We have some young trees directly across the road from us though, so they'll remain this year for us to enjoy all winter.

Our new house is now stained. They put the first coat of stain on early in the week, and it makes a huge difference. We've chosen a fireplace, and changed our minds about the stone for the chimney. I'll leave it to you to guess who wanted to change the stone. We've made a pact that we will not make any more changes to the stone. I'll let you know if we keep it.

We're realizing that here one does not put away summer clothes until very late in the fall. Within twenty-four-hours we can go from T-shirts to turtle necks and sweaters. It happened again this week from Wednesday to Thursday, and then by the week's end, we were back in T-shirts during the afternoons. Luckily, I have summer and winter jeans now, so I'm ready for whatever weather comes along.

I picked up a new hollerism. The guy at the filling station that provides full service to ladies like me filled our tank yesterday and said, "Thank you ladies. You-uns come back again." He pronounced it sort of to rhyme with "prunes." I'm not sure how to spell you-uns but since I'm sure it's not a real word anyway, I won't worry about it.

We're looking forward to a visit from Hope's sister, Faith, and her husband and kids. We're checking out activities for entertaining our niece and nephew so their parents can go look at property in the area. If the weather is good, we're fine. If it's not, the babysitter-in-chief (me) will probably slit her wrists. I'm thinking maybe we can put them to work selling hot chocolate to the Christmas tree seekers. If that doesn't work, we do have Blockbusters here.

We're thankful that all of you have kept in touch with us. We miss you.

Peace and Love,
Leslie and Hope

November 14, 2005

Dear Friends,

I'm still trying to figure out why, when it's twenty degrees out, the holler people don't wear coats. It does warm up to the 40's by afternoon, and the sun is strong, but still, sweatshirts just don't do it when it's that cold.

We're still watching with great fascination as the tree farms prepare for the Christmas season. You'd think we were in Mexico, to look at the fields. All of the migrant workers are here now, working day and night to get the trees cut, wrapped and loaded on the eighteen-wheelers. We're told many of the guys make enough money during the winter tree-cutting season to live comfortably the rest of the year back in Mexico. Several of them also come back for spring planting. It's a mutually beneficial arrangement, because there are not many local folks who want to do that work. Just think, as you vacuum those needles out of your carpet, that your tree might have come from our holler.

There's a project in our town to provide poor children with Christmas gifts, and the organizers especially want books. The group that gets the least attention is pre-teens and teenagers, so, being the good citizen that I am, I went to the store and purchased several books. Most of them are Harry Potter and other types I know will drive the fundamentalists crazy. The children's librarian recommended those titles, so I hope they don't pull them for being un-Christian.

You have no idea just how strong the fundamentalist influence is here. The other day, I was listening to the local radio station, and they were interviewing a woman who runs a spiritual retreat. It sounded very New Age. When the host opened the phone lines to callers, one woman phoned in to chastise the guest for swearing. Both the host and the guest were obviously surprised, because there had been no profanity uttered.

The caller went on to explain that the Bible says you're not supposed to swear, and the guest had said, "I swear it's true," in answer to the interviewer's question. The guest immediately apologized and said, "I'm sorry; I should have said 'I promise it's true,' and the caller self-righteously accepted the apology.

No doubt, the caller will earn extra points for having caught that transgression. Can you believe it? This kind of thing brings out the worst in me, the devil, according to some. My first inclination was to call in and ask if the caller had ever heard of that little item that says you should do unto others as you would have them do unto you, and not embarrass a guest on a radio show. I have no problem with their views; I just wish they wouldn't feel so free to impose them on the rest of us. Amen and hallelujah!

I sometimes wonder why people with such limited tolerance for lots of things, listen to a station that plays country music. You know the themes of those songs. They're mostly about cheating, doing time in prison, and all of those unholy things.

There is one notable exception playing the airwaves these days, though. The new favorite song is one called "Jesus Take the Wheel," about a woman who is driving late at night with her baby in the back seat, when she hits a patch of black ice. Instead of trying to control the car, she throws her hands up and asks Jesus to take over the driving. Now, I've been to the Holy Land, and studied a lot of history, and I know that there were no cars or black ice where Jesus lived, so why she thought he'd be able to do better than she could, is a major question. Anyway, I guess he managed to get the car stopped without anyone getting killed, and she then turned her whole life over to Jesus. And I thought country music was mindless. Shame on me.

Our local library puts on several community interest programs, and yesterday I attended one featuring one of the best known story tellers in Appalachia, a guy named Orville Hicks. He comes from a long line of story tellers, and looks like a real mountain man, with his beard and overalls. He tells stories known as Jack Tales. Their origins are English, as far as anyone knows, and the Scots-Irish settlers of this area brought them from Europe, and have added a mountain touch to them over the centuries. I grew up listening to a Jack tale, and never realized its origin. Jack and the Beanstalk is one.

Hicks mentioned he'd been invited to go to Washington, D.C.

by the Smithsonian, but was reluctant to go. He said they've got lots of story tellers there, and didn't see why they needed him. He was concerned that with some of the outrageous stories some of the politicians tell in Washington, his stories might pale by comparison. They persuaded him to go, though, and as he tells it, he was mighty glad to get back to the mountains.

We're anxiously awaiting the arrival of Faith and Bruce and the two kids. They'll be with us through Thanksgiving. The weather forecast for Monday and Tuesday, the two days I'm babysitting, is not good. I'm hoping for some creative inspiration between now and then. Wish us luck. Enjoy your holiday.

Peace and Love,
Leslie and Hope

- 3 -

First Mountain Winter

December 11, 2005

Dear Friends,

Tree cutting and holiday festivities are in full swing in the holler. We opened the season the day after Thanksgiving with a trip to Blowing Rock with Hope's sister, her husband, Bruce, and the two kids. The town went all out with lighting, Santa, hayrides, free hot chocolate and cider, and a bluegrass band. It was cold but clear, and we managed to get the kids on a hayride. They were expecting a horse drawn wagon but got to ride in the town dump truck filled with hay instead.

We had a lovely Thanksgiving with all the usual trimmings and best of all, a mouse-free house! Brother-in-law Bruce tackled the job, and within three days of his arrival, he had located the probable entry point, sealed it, and carried out too many victims to enumerate. The kids thought it was fun checking the traps every morning and night, just like in the days of the pioneers. Only this was not for food.

We took them to an open bluegrass jam session and we all learned a new song, "Five Pounds of Possum, (in my headlights tonight) about some poor woman whose kids are hungry, and her dog doesn't even have a bone. Her solution to this problem is to run over a possum and feed it to her family. Nice post-Thanksgiving sentiment, don't you think? The kids got lucky with a raffle at the jam, and walked away with three prizes, all of which are loaded with sugar—just what they needed.

Despite constant rain while they were here, we managed to keep the kids occupied. I watched more videos than I'd seen in twenty years. I now know Scooby Doo intimately. I got fairly good at playing Cranium and Clue and know how to say "no" in forty-two different ways. We really enjoyed their visit, but are glad to get back to our quiet lives.

We learned about a new sport this week. Maybe some of you have heard of it, but it was a surprise to us. It's called turkey bowling. They've been doing it here since 1999.

It's exactly what you're thinking. They use a ten-twelve pound frozen turkey instead of a bowling ball. You wrap the bird in duct tape, taking care to maintain its original shape. You can either hold it by the skinny end if your hand is big enough, or just lay the flat part on your hand, and sort of slide it through the air toward the pins. You get three chances, and they add up the points, one for each pin you get down. If you're really good at flipping the bird, so to speak, you can get as much as thirty points. Then the winners get their pictures in the paper. Isn't that exciting?

Winter played with us this week. We were all set, as were the weather pundits, for the first major snow of the season. Forecasts predicted up to ten inches of the white stuff. We dragged out the snow shovels, put in a supply of sand near the door to keep from slipping on the icy steps, and were braced for it.

Nothing happened. About all the shoveling I did was to clean up the mess I made when I knocked over the snow shovels and they upset the pail of sand all over the kitchen floor. We did get a taste of ice though, and realized what a dumb decision our landlord made to have paved the path to the kitchen door with smooth stones. They glazed over like Krispy Kreme doughnuts. It's like competing in an Olympic event, just to get to the car without falling on your butt. I'm trying to figure out how to attach an inflated inner tube to my rear end, so the neighbors will think I'm snow tubing when they see me on the ground in the driveway.

We're constantly learning about new customs here. One bright, sunny morning this week I was at the dump, when I noticed a woman in a fairly new Subaru Outback, unloading her car. What caught my attention was her novel footwear. She had plastic bags on her feet, neatly tied with red ribbons. My first inclination was to feel sorry for her because she had no shoes, but then I remembered the cost of a Subaru, so my worries about her financial straits evaporated. Could this be a seasonal thing with the red ribbons, I wondered. She looked at me and smiled. She must have seen me looking at her feet and I hoped she'd offer some explanation, but she didn't. I guess it was either some sort of fashion statement, or she's germ phobic. If it's the latter, I have to wonder why she didn't have bags on her hands too. Oh well, another holler mystery to be solved.

It's been pretty quiet here this week, so I'll close this. Stay warm.

Peace and Love,
Leslie and Hope

December 18, 2005

Dear Friends,

Every once in awhile I observe something in the holler that nearly defies description. One such vision presented itself one morning as I was driving over to visit our construction site. There was a dead crow, hanging by its neck, in front of a birdhouse that was suspended from a tree limb, in front of someone's house. I was so shocked by it that I stopped the car to get a better look, and sure enough, it was what I thought it was. I couldn't figure out if it was supposed to be a deterrent to other crows, some perverse sort of artistic expression, or just someone's idea of something disgusting to keep visitors away. Have any of you ever seen or heard of this?

We began to see what the locals were talking about with ice storms this week. Old habits die hard, and I couldn't help listening to the school closings on the radio. They close schools at the sign of the first flake or ice crystal. Just as I was wondering how they manage to get in the required number of school days, I saw a signboard outside one of the elementary schools that read, "Saturday school this week." With practically everyone in the holler being Christian, they don't have to deal with diversity issues that would surely crop up in other areas if they tried to have school on Saturday.

I was out at our house the other day when the temperature was in the mid-to low-twenties, and there was a fairly strong wind. I was bundled up in several layers, topped off with a down parka with a hood and ski gloves, dress I thought was appropriate for the weather. The construction crew had other ideas. There they were in their lined Carhart jumpsuits with knit wool caps and no gloves, working as if it were spring.

I guess you do what you have to if you want to make a living. I did what I had to, and went home for a hot cup of tea. There were many times during my working years when I wished I had an outdoor job, like climbing utility poles, where no one would bother me. It's probably a good thing I never got my wish. I'm definitely an indoor person when the temperature dips below freezing.

The plus side to this winter weather is the magnificent mountain scenery. There's a pronounced quiet when everything is blanketed with snow or ice, and it's lovely to enjoy it from inside the warm house. Eventually, when we get deep enough snow, I'll go out and try my new snow shoes. Until then, I've got lots of good books, my banjo and until the power fails, the computer.

I finally do believe that some postal workers observe the motto about "Neither rain, sleet, snow..." In other places we've lived, a half-inch of snow was enough for the mail service to stop for a day or more, so I just thought the slogan was a lot of bull. Here in the holler, though, our intrepid letter carriers not only brave the icy roads, they actually keep pretty much to their regular schedules. I keep looking around for fallen mailboxes to see if they've skidded into the boxes they're trying to fill, but so far there are no signs of mishaps. If they can maneuver on our road, they've got to be good.

We purchased all of our appliances for the new house this week. We bought an extra large capacity washer and dryer, in case we have to start taking in laundry to pay for the place. You never know what the future holds.

The debate over whether it is acceptable to wish people Happy Holidays rather than a Merry Christmas is taking up lots of air time on the local radio station. This is one of those things that's hard to get used to after living in an area where there was general recognition of cultural diversity. I'm somewhat disappointed that despite the introduction of satellite TV and other media that brings world cultures into homes here, people still either refuse to acknowledge the existence of other religions and cultures, or just remain ignorant of their existence. I'm not sure which one I hope is the cause; both are pretty sad.

This week leading up to Christmas, was a time for local businesses to pitch their best wares to holler residents. The big push was on for diabetic socks at People's Drug. It's an interesting commentary on the frequency of diabetes in this area, that they're featuring several diabetic items on sale for the holiday. I'm not sure if it's the level of obesity among poor people, or perhaps a genetic predisposition among the Scots-Irish, or some other factor, but Diabetes is all too prevalent here.

Despite the religious fervor displayed in the "Holiday Greetings" debate, we got invited to a Xmas Eve dinner party. Now that's something I was always taught was a "no-no," to put an "X" in place of Christ, but these people go to church, so I guess it's OK for them to do it. Anyway, it was lovely and our first real holiday celebration in Happy Hollow with our new neighbors. The ride home proved to be pretty harrowing. An accident blocked the only road, and since it was Christmas Eve, we searched in vain for a star to guide us, but found none, so we sat for two hours while they investigated the accident.

We're missing all of you with whom we've spent our holidays during the last twenty years in Maryland. Know that we're sending lots of love as we recall many fun times. Keep us in your thoughts and have happy and safe holidays.

Peace and Love,
Leslie and Hope

January 1, 2006

Dear Friends,

Happy New Year! One of our long-standing traditions is to compile two lists as the year draws to a close. One contains the positive things that have happened to us and those who are closest to us during the year, and the other, as you might guess, is for the negative things that have occurred. Without fail, every year the positive list far outweighs the negative one. We think it's a great way to gain perspective on the year that has just ended. Our plus list will surely include the ties that we forged with all of you and managed to maintain, despite distance and all of our hectic lives.

Also on the plus side is the disappearance of that awful dead crow. Whether some other crows carried it off, or the people who put it there just decided it wasn't a very attractive holiday decoration, we don't know. I'm just glad it's gone.

Our week began Monday with a visit from the famed mountain winds. When it whips itself into a frenzy, the wind can make the snow flurries look like a blizzard. Then, when the wind is taking a breath, all is calm. It's as if someone is turning a switch on and off.

Wind seems to fuel my imagination. I envision all of the cut evergreen trees that are left standing unsold in lots around the country, flying around like whirling dervishes. When the wind gets under the vinyl siding on this house, it emits a sound that's a cross between a cow in labor and a cello madly out of tune. I like it, as long as it doesn't keep me awake at night.

And speaking of things not in tune, we discovered that Hope's new lap harp and my banjo actually can speak to each other. We tried out a few tunes and are convinced if we had more streets in town, we could probably claim one of the corners, and make a few dollars. We're sure people would pay us to stop playing our music.

We had a great time with Joe and Sammy during their two-day visit this week. Sammy, who hails from a place called Hangin' Limb, Tenn., was right at home here. Joe, on the other hand, got a little homesick for the smell of the ocean he has gotten used to in Portland, Maine.

Their visit was quite an educational experience. Sammy taught us lots of American Sign Language words. Some are definitely not for use in polite society, but others are just fine, if we can get them right. It was fun learning to speak his language, sort of like playing charades. I can now add those hand gestures to the ones I learned in New Jersey.

Joan arrived from Atlanta the day after the guys left. We did the obligatory walk-through of our partially completed house and showed her where everything will be when it's finished. She picked out "her" room, as did Joe and Sammy. There's just a small problem; they picked the same one.

We spent New Year's Eve at Sweet Aromas. They had a special dinner, and we enjoyed ourselves before coming home to relax away the final hours of 2005. We've experienced the highs of discovering life in the mountains, and the not-so-high moments that come from missing friends.

We've lost some very dear people along the way this year, and reflect sadly that they didn't live to make the journey into 2006 with us. On balance, though, the year has been one of positive change, and we're happy that 2006 finds us here in North Carolina, embracing a new adventure.

We send our very best wishes to you all for a happy and healthy year ahead. Stay in touch; you're very important to us.

Peace and Love,
Leslie and Hope

January 8, 2006

Dear Friends,

We had an unseasonable thaw this week, making for a very muddy landscape. Our driveway resembled a rice paddy minus the rice, with deep furrows in the mud. Some of those I created trying to get the Camry up the driveway, and some were put there by delivery trucks that couldn't make it up the driveway, and just sat there spinning and spurting mud.

The mail carrier came to our door to ask if we could put more gravel down by the mailbox, because he was sinking so low that he couldn't see into the box. I was about to tell him he didn't need to see in, that he could just reach in, but then I realized he was probably worried about a snake or spider, or some other critter hiding in there.

Feeling sorry for him, I went down to the road with my shovel and engaged in a little "gravel Socialism." I reallocated some gravel from our neighbor's driveway and used it to fill in the gullies by our mailbox. It was for the good of the many, meaning us, to redistribute the gravel from the "haves" to the "have-nots." They're in Florida anyway, so they probably wouldn't mind.

Our log home is starting to come together nicely, and our contractor is just wonderful. She puts up with our millions of questions, our weird notions about what things should cost, and our Yankee ideas about how fast construction should progress. She's also very insistent that the subcontractors do things right, and shows little tolerance when they don't.

When the plumbing supply place delivered the third wrong shower for the guest bathroom, she showed her mettle. She told them if they didn't retrieve the three wrong shower stalls that were standing in the living room; she'd toss them in the dumpster. They had no reason to doubt her, since she'd done exactly that when they left two wrong toilets at her own house. This time, they were taking no chances. As I drove up the road to the construction site, I passed the plumbing supply truck with three rejected shower stalls, enjoying a ride back to the showroom.

For some time, we've wanted to volunteer with the local soup kitchen. We finally made it over there on Saturday, and were surprised to meet someone we know. We discovered it's where the few Democrats in the county can be found. 'Not surprising, when you think about it. We were glad to help out, and our work was welcome. It's nice to be able to do something for folks who have less than we do. Coincidentally, a reporter from the local paper was there, and our picture was taken.

Everyone we meet who is transplanted from somewhere else has the same reaction to the mountains that we do. We all delight in the beauty and pace of living that encourage us to appreciate the simple things: clean air; unbleached water; spectacular scenery; and the most beautiful, star-filled night sky imaginable. We are doing lots of star-gazing these nights.

We're engaged in a new project, selecting door hardware. I admit I never gave it much thought before. My sole experience concerning door hardware involved sticking a wooden matchstick into a stripped hole in a door lock, so I could tighten it. Beyond that, I have always thought of door hardware as purely functional. I am learning now, however, that there is a major aesthetic element to door levers. Hope is my teacher. This has not quite risen to the level of the color wars, but it has definite potential. Don't be surprised if you visit us and notice we have no door hardware.

Just knock and we'll answer. 'Hope to see you soon.

Peace and Love,
Leslie and Hope

January 15, 2006

Dear Friends,

This was the week the Baptists tried to get us. We knew it was coming; it was just a matter of time. It came in an unexpected way, though, and it happened in one of our favorite places, Sweet Aromas. It all started when I recognized a woman whom I'd met at the car dealer, and went over to her table to say "Hello."

During our conversation at the Honda place she had passed along a suggestion for Hope to follow up on in her job search and I thanked her for it. I told her Hope was the woman I'd come in with and she immediately walked over to our table to meet her. As they were getting ready to leave, she and a friend came back over to our table and handed me a card. She thought it would be nice for us to meet other women in the community and invited us to come to her church to hear a great speaker. The card contained the name of the church, the same one that wanted to save us from evolutionists.

In an effort to be polite, I asked what the speaker's topic was, a mistake I will not make again. "Oh, she's giving testimony," my new friend said. "She lost a child and will be telling how she coped with the loss by finding Jesus." I thanked her and said we'd check our schedules.

The flip side of the card had her Avon lady phone number. I was grateful that she didn't invite herself over to give me a makeover, though it surely wouldn't hurt. I just don't think Avon is what I need now. Nor do I need witnessing and testimony.

The holler is all a twitter and the countdown to Nascar season has begun. We get daily bulletins on the drivers and the calendar of events that will launch the season. I'm not totally ignorant of car racing. I have heard of the Daytona 500 and the Indianapolis 500. They're usually pre-empting some program I want to watch. I suspect this is one aspect of holler culture it'll be hard to embrace. I've never enjoyed watching cars crash into each other. It makes me nervous, and reminds me too much of the Washington Beltway and the New Jersey Turnpike.

We now have shingles! No, I'm not talking about the disease. I mean the kind on the roof of our log house. They're fifty-year architectural shingles so I'm hoping I'll never have to replace them. I should be dead and buried by the time they wear out. It's odd to see your mortality reflected in roof shingles, isn't it?

This was another week of big decisions. I hereby proclaim that I did in fact, change my mind. It occurred to me that the kitchen wall, the decorative tile on it and the color we selected for our cabinets, looked horrible together. That's an understatement. It made me want to puke. Rather than look at something that would aggravate and nauseate us for the rest of our lives, we made some dramatic changes. We changed cabinets, stain color, and cabinet makers, and went for a whole new look.

Off we went with our contractor to meet with a new designer for five hours, over two days, deciding on design, color and configuration for the kitchen cabinets. And amazingly, we saved money by making the change.

Lamps we ordered for the living room tables arrived, and joined the rest of our stuff in the attic. If we get out of this adventure without hernias, it will be a miracle. I don't think we ordered anything that weighs less than fifty pounds, and I'm not a whole lot of help when the weight pushes past twenty pounds. Poor Hope has to be the pack mule. There are definite advantages to having a partner who is younger, stronger and lots taller than I am.

Building a home can be a very humbling experience. We've shown our ignorance to so many people, in so many ways, that we are probably the laughing stock of the holler. If we had any pride about our intellects, that went by the wayside about two years ago.

Some of the things we don't know astound even us. We're grateful our contractor doesn't laugh at us when we exhibit stupidity like we did the other day. We had purchased a brass pinecone door-knocker and doorbell to match about a year ago. It never occurred to us that the doorbell plate had to have something attached to make that ding-dong sound. I just thought it got put on the door, and there'd be sound when you pushed the button. Some of you will probably find this funny, and others are probably wondering what the hell I'm talking about. You're the ones who can sympathize with us. We're still quite worthy of the moniker, The Two Stooges Construction Company.

We are aware that certain stereotypes of mountain people, especially those in the holler, can be quite offensive, so we're careful not to use any expressions that might be hurtful. Despite our care not to offend, sometimes we see and hear things that are just too funny not to share. One such example surfaced when I was using the local telephone directory to find the name of a business. As I let my fingers do the walking, I glanced at the top of a page to see the heading, "Trailer-Trash."

Now, I know they didn't mean that the way it sounds, but it struck me funny. It's one of those things I'm guessing the editors of the phone book missed. 'Sort of like the McDonald's ad in the Help Wanted section that boasted, "People are our most important ingredient." Hmmm, got a craving for a big Mac lately?

On that note, I have to scrounge up some lunch. Until next update, stay warm.

Peace and Love,
Leslie and Hope

February 5, 2006

Dear Friends,

I'm back in the holler following a trip to Florida and more convinced than ever that I'm really a mountain woman. I had a great time visiting my cousins and some dear friends, but I kept looking around for something taller than I was. The landfill that lays claim to being the highest point in southern Florida just didn't give me the same feeling these mountains do. I'm glad to be back "up mountain."

When I returned, I learned I'd missed a major event. According to a story in *The Mountain Times* this week, Lucy, the cat, had a 20th birthday party, complete with cake. This occasion warranted two photos. Now, before you all decide to send all of your elderly animals here to claim their fifteen minutes of fame, consider that our per diem rate for animals is $5,000, enough to cover the cost of oxygen and emergency room care for me, when I have a severe allergic reaction to the critters.

You will not believe what movie we saw in the holler the other night—"Brokeback Mountain." Yes, this moving love story involving two cowboys really came to the holler. As we approached the theater, I held my breath, fearing the marquee would read "Homo on the Range," and that there'd be Bible-toting picketers, but the audience seemed to appreciate the film as much as we did, and there were no picket signs.

Hope has informed me that it's a "job" she's seeking now, rather than a "position." When we first arrived in the holler, she was trying to land a position. As proof of her evolution as a mountain woman, recognizing the futility of locating a professional position, it's now a full-fledged job hunt. She's had three interviews this week, one of which was a second interview, so we're keeping fingers and toes crossed that she'll get an offer.

We decided to go ahead and purchase the rest of our furniture before another natural disaster forces prices higher. We bought the rest of our living room furniture and got a free set of stoneware. I felt like a kid again, going to the Roosevelt Theater to see a double feature, and bringing home a free dish to add to the collection of eclectic "China" we had. These dishes are a step up from the Melmac and jelly glasses of yesteryear; in fact they are quite nice.

You're all aware that this was the week that the little beady-eyed prognosticator gave his view of the future and also that it was Groundhog Day. As to the former, I couldn't bring myself to watch the State of the Union speech, but I did read it in *The Washington Post* online. If I were a wealthy, oil-owning munitions manufacturer, I guess I'd rejoice in anticipation of more war and tax cuts. Short of that, I saw nothing to fuel any optimism for the country.

As if to underscore the state of things, our friend Joan has already decided that when she's retired and living in Philadelphia, she will head for the holler at the first sign of a nuclear attack, and has already reserved her room. I know how she feels. I must acknowledge that I feel much safer since moving to the mountains. I no longer experience the same degree of stress when the feds raise the security level, as I did when we lived a stone's throw from Washington and the National Security Agency.

Of course, I also recognize that the old saw, "Ignorance is bliss" is even truer when I don't read a newspaper or listen to news for two or three days. After working in public relations all those years, and being glued to local, state and national news, it's still part of my decompression process. I could form a 12-step program for recovering news junkies. I'll bet there are others out there doing the same thing.

Since I'm on a political tear, let me also note how pleased I was to see Dr. Johnetta Cole take Rev. Joseph Lowery to task for his comments on the passing of Coretta Scott King. He praised King for her roles as wife and mother, while ignoring her contributions to the human rights movement. Dr. Cole reminded him and viewers of Jim Lehrer's News Hour that Mrs. King walked beside her husband, not behind him. Lowery tried to recover, but he was definitely left with much-deserved egg on his face. 'Nuff said.

Language is so important. We think we're doing pretty well with it in the holler, but every now and then we run into something really challenging. I saw two guys in a truck pull into our driveway and walked out to greet them. The conversation went like this. Guy #1:

"Hey, we're workin' on the pump house over yonder. Kin I bar yer par?" Me: Blank stare. Guy #1: Ah kin plug it in over thar (pointing to an outside outlet) Me: (Suddenly realizing he was asking if he could borrow our electricity) "Sure, help yourself." I have learned that if I don't answer people, they'll realize I didn't understand them and provide some additional clues. It's sort of like being on a game show but without the prizes.

Keep yer par crankin'.

Peace and Love,
Leslie and Hope

February 12, 2006

Dear Friends,

This was a real winter week here. We never got much above the low 40's, and the wind chill pushed the "feels like" temperature into the single digits a few times. It didn't stop us from appreciating a beautiful, clear sky at night, though. It's like being in a planetarium when you walk outside after dark. I especially love the moonlight, because it allows me to walk outside at night and not worry about falling over something. Night blindness has always kept me from enjoying walking in the dark. With a light coating of snow on the hillsides this week, it reflected even more light, and made me think I was in a Vincent Van Gogh painting.

On Saturday we awakened to real snow, the first of any notable amount since we came to the holler. It looked like someone placed a blanket of cotton on top of the evergreens. My reverie was interrupted by the sound of the radio announcer cautioning people to avoid the secondary roads. I didn't know we had anything but secondary roads.

I used to think people in the D.C.-Baltimore corridor were a bit strange about snow, particularly when some of them would get hysterical at the first sign of a flake. I figured these tough mountain people would just go about their business and not let snow interfere with their routines. Boy, was I wrong. Ice is often the hidden hazard and with curvy mountain roads, caution is always the rule.

Even before the first flake appears, as soon as snow creeps into the forecast, school gets cancelled. As a sign of just how careful they are when it snows, this morning I heard numerous announcements of cancelled Sunday school and other church activities. Let me tell you. If church is cancelled, you know it's deadly serious in the holler.

We had all of four to five inches of snow, I'd guess, between yesterday and last night. The roads were nearly empty yesterday, and again today. 'No need for Jesus to be taking over too many steering wheels today. The one thing they don't do here is abandon cars in the middle of the road, like they do along Routes 50 and 95 in Maryland. These folks are smarter. They just stay home.

The weather was perfect for an indoor musicale this week. I dusted off my banjo and convinced Hope to get out her lap harp. We did fine with "On Top of Old Smoky" and "Amazing Grace," but got hung up on "Home on the Range." Hope's repertoire extends only to those songs that come on cards with circles on them that tell you where you're supposed to pluck the strings. I've urged her to practice, so maybe we can go out and get a gig somewhere and make a few dollars. We could introduce a whole new category of music, Inept Rustic.

I saw a new sign this week that I'd never seen. It had a black circle with a red diagonal line through the words "dipping and chewing." It was on the elementary school building where we go to help with the soup kitchen. Next to it was another circle with the "no smoking" message. The chewing and dipping refers to tobacco and snuff, and they obviously don't want the kids using either in school. You'd never know anyone was trying to discourage its use though, judging from the prominent displays of those products in stores. I never knew there were so many different things to chew and stick up your nose.

That's all from the holler this week. Stay warm and dry and watch your backs with that snow shoveling.

Peace and Love,
Leslie and Hope

February 19, 2006

Dear Friends,

We went from winter to spring and back again, this week. By Wednesday nearly all of the snow had melted. At Happy Hollow, where they had a bit more snow, it was nearly gone too. The sun is so strong at this altitude; it really warms things up when it stays around for awhile. I was walking around in a turtleneck and sweatshirt Tuesday, Wednesday and Thursday. That's my dress-up outfit for warm winter days.

Our new house is awash in color. We worried that the colors we selected would not look like the samples, since they rarely do. Well, they must have improved the technology used in producing samples, because every color is right on the money. We couldn't be more pleased, and while I thought I'd never believe it, the color wars were worth it after all.

The other night as we were leaving the Hollow to drive back to West Jefferson, we ran into some unexpected traffic. We were forced to sit and wait while some of the locals drank their fill at the neighborhood watering hole. I know what you're thinking and you're wrong. The locals in this instance were ducks that inhabit one of the yards on the road leading to the Hollow. And the watering hole was a pothole filled with snowmelt. It's not the first time these birds have held us up. They sometimes decide to just stand in the road, and you have to wait until their leader, a testy rooster, calls them away. It's fun to watch them, though, so we don't usually mind the delay.

I had one of those flashbacks from my youth on Friday night. I ran out to get a battery for our clock and noticed several people sitting in their cars in the store parking lot. I was curious so I turned off the motor and sat and watched. Apparently, this is one of the local cruising spots. Cars full of teenage boys pull up next to cars filled with teenage girls and they grunt at each other through the open car windows. It looks like some of the mating rituals I've seen on the TV nature programs. Come to think of it, from the youthful appearance of many of the mothers I've seen dragging toddlers

104

around, that's probably exactly what I witnessed.

Two guys who are also building at Happy Hollow stayed with us this weekend. On Sunday morning, as we were all having breakfast together, Hope's sister called to catch up on family drama. Suddenly, in the middle of their conversation she stopped and asked Hope, "Do you have men there?" She had heard the guys talking, and it was breakfast time, and well, you can guess what she was thinking, or I should say, hoping. I told Hope to tell her we'd all found Jesus and were going straight, but Hope is too sensible to listen to me, so she ignored my advice.

We went to a great bluegrass concert the other night. East Tennessee State University has a major in bluegrass studies, and they have a great band that tours the area, including Mountain City, Tennessee, where we saw it. I'd love to sit in on some of the classes at the university. It would be fascinating to see if academia can turn bluegrass music into something theoretical and dull.

By now, you surely know that there are some basic differences between life in the mountains and life as we lived it elsewhere. The challenge for us is to try to acclimate and hasten our assimilation into rural Appalachian life. One example of a difference caught my attention when I stopped at the local CVS pharmacy to retrieve a prescription. I was surprised to see a handwritten note tacked on the front door saying the pharmacy was closed due to illness, and they weren't sure when it would reopen. I got concerned that maybe the much-feared bird flu pandemic had arrived, and we hadn't heard about it. I figured it must be pretty serious for a pharmacy to be closed.

We later learned they don't have a backup pharmacist, and when one gets sick they just close down. Fortunately for me, I've maintained the good old New Jersey habit of hording drugs, so I wasn't in danger of running out of anything critical. It did strike me as a bit strange, though.

Hope continues her job search. She had to take a psychological profile test the other day and found some of the questions shocking. One asked if the applicant thought she could refrain from using cocaine before coming to work. We guessed they don't care if you use it after work. Another one asked if you thought it was OK to steal $0, $5, $10 or $25. They also wanted to know how many times in the past year she'd had fistfights with co-workers. Can you just imagine the kinds of questions they'd ask if this had been a Las Vegas casino or nightclub? We don't have those in the holler. This was just a retail store.

I'm sure glad I never had to take a test like that. This irrepressible urge seems to overtake me when I get into those situations. I get a terrible attack of smartassitis. I'm sure I'd have put down that I often attack human resources managers when I don't get hired. We guess Hope passed the test, but there aren't any jobs available now. That's too bad. She's certainly well qualified. She doesn't snort cocaine and she doesn't steal, and I can fall over laughing trying to visualize her in a fistfight.

Please let us hear from you. Now that the Olympics are over, you can get back to email. We miss all of you.

Peace and Love,
Leslie and Hope

March 5, 2006

Dear Friends,

Our education about small town life continues. We've been told by several people that everyone here knows everyone else, so we need to be careful what we say about anyone. For example, the plumber who fixes things in this house is the father of the man who built it. He is also the minister of the church that the father of our landlord attends. Did you follow all of that? The more people we meet, the more we realize how true this is.

The thing about six degrees of separation operates on an even more intimate level here. Not only do all of the people here seem to know each other, they also know all about each other's business. Given all of this, we're sure the people of West Jefferson now know more about our business than most of you do.

I had to laugh when our landlord was here for the first time. She was praising us for taking such good care of her house. She let me know that she had been particularly impressed when the plumber (also the minister of her father's church) told her that he'd come to fix a leaky kitchen sink and found something pretty remarkable.

Only one side of the double sink was leaking so I put a piece of bright yellow duct tape across the tub on the leaky side, so we wouldn't forget and use it by mistake. When he saw the tape, he asked about it, and I explained its purpose. He said nothing, but was obviously impressed enough to tell a member of his flock, who then told his daughter, the landlord. "That," she assured me, "tells me what kind of people you are and how careful you're being with our house." How about that? We can add this to the many uses of duct tape—positive PR.

Since I had some prescription bottles on the bathroom sink one other time when the plumber was here, I can now assume that everyone in town knows my medical history as well. I'm sure he also noted two alarm clocks on either side of the king-sized bed, and that there were no photos or statues of Jesus in the house. Slice it any way you want it, and that can only mean one thing; heathen sinners live here.

This connectedness thing was reinforced recently when we attended a party at the home of the minister who runs the soup kitchen where we volunteer. Watching the conversation was like piecing together a jigsaw puzzle. Within minutes, it became apparent that the few people who didn't know one another, all knew people in common, except for us, of course. Five minutes after we got there they were all connected. It seldom takes more than one or two questions before they discover common relatives or friends. It's like a search for the extended kinship link. In New Jersey, we called that Jewish geography.

I found myself in conversation with three people who home school their kids, a popular thing in the holler. These women all seemed reasonably intelligent and one was actually a certified teacher. When I commented that I'm always surprised to see school-aged children in the stores during normal school hours, they assured me that the one-on-one teaching that goes on in their homes is so much more efficient than what happens in a public school classroom with thirty kids, that it's perfectly OK for the kids to be shopping with their parents during the day. One even suggested that three days a week is enough to cover the curriculum with home schooling.

As you might imagine, I was ready to burst with comments I dared not make. I learned from them that the qualification required of a parent to home school kids in NC is a high school diploma. Imagine that, in this nation so consumed with No Child Left Behind requirements for "highly qualified" teachers in every public classroom. Something's seriously out of whack here.

I'd seen a thirteen year-old boy helping his father lay tile in the bathroom of our house last week, and when I asked if it was a school holiday he told me he was being home schooled. His father was quick to assure me that the boy spends three days a week at home with his mother and on the other two, he is learning to lay tile. "That way," he said, "when he's 18, I won't have to worry about him." I've got news for him. If it takes this kid five years to learn to lay tile, his father had better start worrying about him now.

This is pretty hard stuff for me to swallow as a former teacher, and it's hard to refrain from asking them how these kids will ever be able to work with others, especially those who are different from themselves. In the old days when I worked for a teacher's union and was asked about home schooling, I was able to sound off about the inherent weaknesses of it, but now I have to remember that shooting off my mouth could result in cockeyed tile on my walls or worse.

Peace and Love,
Leslie and Hope

March 12, 2006

Dear Friends,

I'm sure you've heard the old saw about March coming in like a lion. Well, here in the holler, it seems like the entire pride brought the month in. We had winds up to fifty miles per hour the other night. I looked for Dorothy and Toto, but didn't see them.

On Wednesday, I was able to confirm that the finish carpenters who were supposed to be here two weeks ago are indeed real. I'd started to wonder if they were a figment of our contractor's imagination. They are real, and as a matter of fact, when I showed up and asked them if I could take their picture for a slide show I'm preparing, they got all "Hollywood." 'Had to take their caps off and slick down their hair to look just right. Imagine if I'd walked in with a video camera. It was great to watch them work. There's real artistry in what they do.

It is so pretty here that I sometimes have to stop and ask myself if I'm really living here. The other day as I drove along the New River, I just had to get out and walk around to appreciate the scenery. The rushing river spoke of the coming of spring, while the overhanging snow-covered pine boughs told quite a different tale. The scenery here always seems to weave a tapestry of contrasts, with seasons never quite being able to make up their minds whether to come or go.

I wonder if I've just never taken the time to see these things, or if they just didn't show up in the urban settings where I've lived until now. I'm very grateful that I've reached a time in life when I can take the time to absorb the beauty of my surroundings.

Not everything I spend time on these days is so idyllic. I also have time now to go after businesses that try to rip me off. I'm absolutely convinced that companies get away with producing shoddy products because they know people are too busy to take the time to return them or complain.

Hope has long referred to me as a Ninja consumer, knowing how pissed off I get when someone is trying to cheat me. She'll have to come up with a new term, now that I'm retired, because now I have

110

even more time to let those who sell me crappy merchandise know of my displeasure. I could easily make a career of offering offending companies the opportunity to make amends for my aggravation. I've discovered that if I send a brief email regarding some inferior product, what often accompanies an apology is a coupon so I can get even more of the crummy product, but at no cost.

This week I was on a roll. I took on the company that sold me a king-sized quilt that turned out to be prince-sized. When I called and talked to the customer service person, I was told I'd have to pay for the return shipping. I said I doubted that would happen. I asked her to inquire about whether they wanted me to pay to return the quilt, and then send out a news release to their competitors to use as they saw fit. Perhaps, I suggested, they'd rather pay the return postage so I could get a refund. They wisely chose the latter.

The second target of my consumer ire this week was the company that makes Brillo. I opened a box the other night to find a blue blob of steel wool that looked like it had been run over and dragged by an Amtrak train. The quality control folks were clearly out to lunch on that one, so I emailed the company and told them. I offered them a digital photo as proof. Digital photography is a wonderful tool in the Ninja consumer's arsenal, I've discovered. They're sending me a coupon for another box of mangled Brillo pads.

I've just learned that the concept of "southern gentlemen" is a myth. There was a time when men in the South would jump to their feet when a lady entered the room, and wouldn't dream of allowing her to lift heavy objects, or in any other way risk breaking a sweat. Childbirth would be the obvious exception to this, naturally. I thought, based on the full service for ladies at the gas station, that this was still the case. Well, as experience showed, clearly, I was wrong.

We loaded up both of our cars and our contractor's truck with things to take to the new house and headed for Happy Hollow. Nicole assured us the guys would carry the stuff into the house for us. Once we got there and began carrying in heavy boxes, the three guys stayed on their behinds and continued eating their lunches and gabbing. We emptied the truck and started unloading the first car. Still they sat. Nicole suggested to them that they could work off their lunches by helping us. One man got up to help, but the others stayed seated.

While we were at the car picking up more boxes, I saw Nicole close the front door. When I carried in the next box, I saw she had the three guys in another room, and was talking to them. As if by magic, they all shot out of that room and scurried to carry in the rest of the boxes. Nicole ordered us not to lift another thing. I can only guess what that southern lady had to say to them, and I suspect it wasn't very ladylike.

Her ladyship has to sign off now. Take care and let us hear from you.

Peace and Love,
Leslie and Hope

March 19, 2006

Dear Friends,

Some of you may recall that I had my heart set on a taxicab yellow SUV when we moved to the holler. I was sure it would come in handy if Hope got stuck in a snowdrift en route home from work one night. Sadly, I ended up having to settle for a tan one, since all the yellow SUVs were like big trucks. To satisfy my craving for bright yellow in my life, I convinced Hope to let me choose that color for the inside of the garage in the new house. She was so relieved about not having to drive a yellow car, she agreed. This week, we finally saw the yellow garage, and it's beautiful! The most generous concession I could squeeze out of Hope was that it wasn't as bad as she thought it would be, and it looked cheerful.

Hope attended a training session on family violence this week, because of her continuing interest in that issue. When I asked her how it went, she told me she was somewhat shocked when a law enforcement official attending the seminar asked the presenter under what circumstances strangling is permissible in a domestic dispute. She's hoping he was just inarticulate, and didn't really mean it the way it sounded.

Nine months after moving to the holler I'm still finding the local radio station a veritable treasure chest of information. One tidbit I picked up this week was, according to the local disc jockey, Night Rider is a target of a takeover by another media outlet. I was sure I misheard him, but listened carefully as he repeated, "Night Rider." For a brief moment I wondered whether the Ku Klux Klan was now in the media business. Given some of the right wing extremists that have talk shows, it wouldn't have been too surprising. Then I realized he was talking about Knight-Ridder, the publisher of several major U.S. newspapers. I resisted the temptation to call the station to correct his pronunciation, wondering if it was a Freudian slip.

We're about six weeks out from completion of our house, and our contractor has started talking to us about landscaping. We're tempted to put a moat around the house to keep the creditors at bay, but that's hard to do on the side of a mountain. Besides, we didn't put a drawbridge into the plans.

In addition to the "ladyship" that was bestowed upon me by a local filling station, I've also been recognized for my honesty by another one. There's a small gas station/grocery store that sits just about midway between the holler and our new house, and I stop there from time to time when I'm starving and need a quick chocolate fix, or bottle of water. It's not the kind of place you'd buy anything that wasn't wrapped, if you get the picture.

There's a sign on the pump that says, "Pay first before pumping," so I went in and gave the guy money before pumping gas. When I went back in to get my change, he told me I didn't need to pay first, because he knew I was honest. He volunteered the information that sometimes people from Tennessee come by and pump gas, and then come in and tell him they have no money, and that's why the sign is up. This isn't the first time I've detected a bias against people from the adjoining state. It made me feel good to have him note that I didn't look like a gas thief, or a Tennessean, for that matter. Dolly Parton and Davy Crockett, forgive me.

Just when I thought my drafting days were over, our contractor reminded us that we have to have closet plans. We've never had closets big enough to require plans before, and we never had any say in how they were designed anyway, so this is virgin territory for us. I got out my graph paper, calculator, ruler and colored pencils, and went to work. I think it took nearly as long to design a walk-in closet, as it did to design the whole house.

We got it done, and I took immense pleasure in being able to design it to scale. I love to envision the face of the geometry teacher who flunked me in high school. I'll bet some of her pet students couldn't do this. Wherever you are, Hazel Farquaher, if you haven't already turned over in your grave, this should give you the boost you need.

We went to a St. Patrick's Day party at the home of one of our Happy Hollow neighbors Friday night. It was great fun, and I got to put on my green overalls again. There are at least two or three occasions a year when they are appropriate. Wearing my recent title of Domestic Diva ever so proudly, I baked a cake, and even managed to give it a green topping. I knew that leftover paint would come in handy.

Our menu for the party reminded me of the old days at Barringer High School in Newark when the Italian kids would deliberately wear orange on St. Patrick's Day, just to get in the faces of the few Irish kids. We had pizza at the St. Pat's party!

We're trying to stay grounded despite the enormous excitement about the house being finished. It's really hard to focus much on anything else, but we do think of you and imagine you visiting us in the new place. We can't wait for you to see it and us.

Peace and Love,
Leslie and Hope

- 4 -

The Long Journey Home

March 26, 2006

Dear Friends,

I am so impressed with people who can build a house from scratch. Our builder is amazing. His talent is boundless. However, the subcontractors who are supposed to make the house livable are not always up to his level.

For instance, one day this week we discovered that the electricians installed two flush-mounted lights on a slanted ceiling. We never bothered to tell them we were expecting the lights to hang straight so they hung them flush with the slanted ceiling at about a forty-five degree angle. When I walked down the hall and looked at those lights I felt like I was on the Titanic as it was going down. I thought I'd have to live the rest of my life on Dramamine. The lights have since been straightened out, but the guys were surprised we didn't care for them the way they'd hung them. I guess they think we're too picky.

Sometimes they get a little too creative, as I noted the other day when I saw a single sconce fixture smack in the middle of the only sheetrock wall in the living room. The plans showed it clearly in the lower corner to illuminate the stairs leading to the basement, but the electrician told me he thought it looked better there. I had to break the news to him that he wasn't the one to make that decision, and all we expected was that he'd follow the very detailed plans the contractor gave him. It's been moved and the wall was patched and repainted. He acted very hurt about the whole thing.

The plumbers get artsy too from time to time. One decided it would look good to mount the wall shower fixture in the corner, instead of the middle of the wall. Of course, I didn't see it until the tile was already placed around it, so I let it stay. We might start a new trend in the holler, naughty girl showers where you get to stand in the corner.

I know we don't have a monopoly on weird weather here in the holler, but this week was a doozy. On Monday, the first day of spring, I saw two robins sitting in snow on our driveway, looking at each other. It was a perfect scene for a comic strip. The little bubble above their heads could have said, "Did I turn the wrong page of the calendar?" or just plain, "Happy spring."

On Friday, we got another chance to socialize with our local holler neighbors at a free concert at the library. The place was packed, and we soon realized we were the only ones who had to work at understanding some of the jokes. It took a few minutes to realize why everyone was laughing when they introduced one of the band members as a local pharmacist and made some reference to him supplying the band with what sounded like Vagar. After a few more references to Vagar, we got enough contextual clues to realize they were talking about Viagra.

There was another comment made about one of the musicians learning he was kin to some famous southern figure, on both sides of his family. The audience thought that was a real knee-slapper, an obvious reference to the past occurrence of inbreeding in the mountains. That's an example of a joke that the mountain people can tell to each other but it would be frowned upon if we referred to the practice.

Also during the introductions, they said one guy was from L.A. and we assumed that meant Los Angeles. Nope, around here that refers to Lansing, a small town we were told we probably didn't want to live in.

As we were leaving the concert, we heard several people saying goodbye, all using the same expression, "You'uns (pronounced yunz) get home safe now," or "See all you'uns later." It took me from 1985 to about 2000 to get rid of my New Jersey "yiz" and bring myself to say "y'all." I doubt I have enough years left on this planet to bring me to "you'uns."

You know how we used to sit around and swap war stories about difficult employees we had to supervise? Well, we heard one the other day that had a real local tint to it. Someone was telling us one of her employees didn't show for work one day this week, never called or anything, and walked in the next day with this excuse.

It seems she'd been at a moonshine party the night before with her eighteen-year-old sister and the sister's boyfriend. The sister is nine months pregnant, and for that reason wasn't drinking moonshine. She's health-conscious and that's a good thing. The boyfriend got plastered and had the pregnant girlfriend drive him home. He needed to toss his cookies en route, so she let him out to hang over a ditch. Feeling sorry for him, she got out to see if he was OK. He recovered quickly enough to jump back in the truck and took off, leaving her stranded on the side of the road at 4 a.m. The AWOL employee got a call from her stranded sister and had to go get her, and that's why she didn't come to work. Now that's the kind of excuse that leaves the boss speechless.

You'uns take care and keep in touch, now. See, it just doesn't sound right coming from me, does it?

Peace and Love,
Leslie and Hope

April 2, 2006

Dear Friends,

This was one of our most hectic weeks since our arrival in the holler last summer. As they say around the mountains, we've been as busy as two moths in a mitten. Once again, our home resembles a warehouse after a clearance sale. We've begun packing in earnest for the eventual move into our log home. It's a very good feeling to know that this will be our last step in the journey we began five and a half years ago, when we bought land in Happy Hollow. Now that it's imminent, we can hardly contain our excitement.

Tuesday was particularly nerve-wracking. Hope got a call for a second interview with the organization she really hoped would hire her. We guessed the second interview was a good sign, that she wasn't being called back so they could tell her she wouldn't be hired, but you never know. She's come so close to being hired before, only to find out somebody had a cousin who got hired instead. Understandably, we were trying not to get too excited.

She left here at 10:30 and I started watching the clock. Her appointment was for 11. By 1:30 when she still wasn't home I didn't know what to think. I figured she might have gotten an offer and started working already. I also considered the option that things had gone sour, and she'd gone off in search of a bar. Since this is a dry county, that could take awhile. I packed six boxes of glassware, hoping that would make the time go faster, but it didn't. I'd once heard that chocolate is a mood booster, so I ate a dish of chocolate pudding to calm my nerves, but all that did was make me want more.

Mercifully, before I could dive into the second dish of pudding, Hope pulled into the driveway. I ran out to greet her and she announced she was starting her new job on Monday. What a relief for both of us!

We're both very grateful for the support you've lent during this time of Hope's unemployment. Obviously, we didn't expect it to take so long for her to land a job. We're happy that I don't have to start working again. I'm now assigned to finalize the details with the new house and then get it organized, and that's just fine. Now the long list of "When Hope Gets a Job" items gets pulled out of the drawer and we'll be tackling that. As they say in the southern mountains, "This is gooder 'n grits." I'm assuming that means pretty good, but since I can't stand grits, I'll have to take it on faith, and you know there's no shortage of that around here.

Speaking of local expressions, we learned a new one this week and it's a good thing it was explained to us. If you offer somebody something and they say, "I don't care to" it means "I don't mind if I do" or "Yes, thank you." I was assuming that it was a refusal and I'm wracking my brains trying to think if I heard that at the soup kitchen and didn't give somebody soup who really wanted it. I sure hope not.

Our contractor says we'll be able to get a certificate of occupancy for the new house in a week. I know better than to take that literally; I'm betting on two weeks. Once we get the certificate, we can decide when we'll do the actual move into the house.

To celebrate all of these great events, we both got haircuts on Saturday and polished off what was left of an apple pie Hope made. Now I have to fast for two days to get into my jeans.

Spring is definitely coming to the holler. Trees are budding, grass is greening, and I've worn T-shirts three times this week, all sure signs that it is around the bend. Hope you're having a good start to my favorite season. Now, I must get back to the packing.

Peace and Love,
Leslie and Hope

April 9, 2006

Dear Friends,

We began this week by constructing our "punch list" for the contractor. I'm not sure what the derivation of the term is; we're a bit puzzled by it. We can't figure out whether we're the puncher or the punchee. Does the builder punch the client for having so many complaints, or does the client punch the builder for all of the screw-ups? I guess we'll find out. It's really a shame we have to do this. The house is beautiful and it's a real bummer that we have to go looking for things that are wrong. We'll do it, though, because we know if they don't get fixed now, we'll have to pay later for them to get corrected.

We continue to marvel at how well our contractor controls her temper when dealing with the electricians, one of whom I've taken to calling "two shoes," which is short for "two shoes full of stupid." That's an expression we heard a friend use several years ago and I thought it was a bit of overkill. In this case, sadly, it's probably understatement. For the record, if our new home burns down and we're not around to tell about it, someone please get the boys from Jersey to go after the electricians. They probably don't have much money, but our souls will rest easier knowing they at least suffered broken kneecaps.

With the start of this official first work week for Hope, I'm now realizing another goal I had set for retirement. I'm now officially a "kept" woman. What remains to be seen, is whether she can keep me in the style to which I have become accustomed. Come to think of it, if we use recent months as an indicator, that shouldn't be hard. Not that I have anything against peanut butter and jelly, mind you, but it gets a bit boring after ten months.

I thought I could take a day off to enjoy my new status and not go to our house. I realized Monday that wasn't a good option. I wasn't going to go out there, but after a conversation with our contractor, I changed my mind. It was a good thing I showed up. Nicole greeted me with this question, "Are you ready?" I've learned that's her way of preparing us for bad news. "Lay it on me," I replied, and she did.

The wall oven didn't fit into the cabinet we'd had custom made for it. I had only two questions: "Why?" and "How do we get it to fit?" We did figure out a solution with the carpenters, and it will delay the completion of the kitchen, of course, but it will be workable and look good. It wouldn't surprise me if the designer who did the custom cabinets ends up selling shoes somewhere. Nicole still plans to go for a certificate of occupancy this Friday. 'Got to admire her tenacity. After this experience, I decided I'd better show up at the house every day. There's too much excitement, and I wouldn't want to miss any crises.

There are still some diversions to take my mind off the house. People here are generally very appreciative of the natural beauty that surrounds us and rarely do you see people littering or in any way trashing the landscape. Knowing this, the other day when I drove past the nearby pasture, and saw about forty empty beer bottles strewn around in the grass, I could only come to one conclusion. The cows are partying hard! As further evidence of their wild ways, I noted they were nowhere to be seen. I imagined the lot of them lying around the barn with ice packs on their heads. Either they'd been grounded for their trashy behavior, or they were partying late last night because they knew today was the day they were to take the long last ride to the slaughterhouse.

We passed a major milestone on Friday with the house. No, we didn't get the certificate of occupancy; the inspector never showed. The milestone I'm referring to is that I learned how to turn the water on and off in the house, and that means we no longer have to use a Port-a- John outside. We've also set a tentative moving date of May 5th, and that's about as exciting as it can get.

Rest assured, as busy as we'll be in the coming weeks, as we're getting the house in order, we'll be thinking of how soon you can come to visit us in our new digs. Take care and let us hear from you. We'll email you the new address and phone number.

Peace and Love,
Leslie and Hope

April 16, 2006

Dear Friends,

Our week got off to a great start with receipt of our certificate of occupancy on Monday. We wasted no time and packed up one of the cars and took boxes over to the house that very night. We had a couple of days to bring things over before they started sanding and finishing the wood floors. Once that started, the place was such a mess that we were restricted to the basement.

We continue to have "adventures" with the workers. At the same time we got the good news about passing inspection, we also learned one of the carpenters lost his balance and landed on the cook top with a very heavy shoe. It broke and has to be replaced. At least we won't have to worry about the first damage to the kitchen. It's already been through hell and we haven't even had a shot at it. The carpenters did figure out a way to get the wall oven into the cabinet, by the way, so except for replacing the cook top, the kitchen is nearly done.

Lots of people are taking off the weekend for Easter and several community activities are planned. If I have time, I want to be sure to get to the local pet store that has been advertising a special event. They claim to be the only authorized Harley pet wear dealer in the area. I can't wait to see the bunnies in leather!

We've been getting estimates for the move to the new house. When I asked about insurance, one guy told me, "You have to expect something to get damaged in a move." His honesty was refreshing, but you can guess who won't be getting the job.

We're gearing up for primary elections here, and so many people are running for Clerk of the Court and Sheriff, it's hard to know who should get our votes. There's Willie Brown who's running for sheriff on a platform of "A Fresh Start," which is terribly appropriate for him, since he's a convicted felon. NC law allows felons to run for office but not vote. Then there's Rufus Green who's running for Clerk of the Court and promises to carry out his "physical" responsibilities to serve the people of Ashe County. Hmm, I wonder what those might be.

We got our first taste of mountain home ownership this week, even before moving in. Our sensor lights over the garage and on the front of the house went haywire and remained on for six days. By the time I discovered this, I'm sure the electric bill went into triple digits. With the help of five people, I climbed up the tallest ladder I've ever been on and shut them off. I knew if I fell, one or two of our new friends would have caught me. I need to get used to tall ladders; that's the only way we'll be able to clean the rafters in the living room. Don't look up when you come to visit.

We're having dinner today at Happy Hollow with friends. In my honor, the Easter ham will be joined by an Easter chicken. I told them I'd be perfectly content to eat chocolate bunnies and jelly beans, but they insisted on doing the chicken. Shoot! That's the new word around here, by the way. Hope says everyone in her office uses it. She needs to get in the habit of substituting vowels so they don't think she's vulgar.

We're exhausted from packing and carrying things, but happy in the knowledge that this will be our last move. I swear I'm never going to leave this house unless I go feet first. 'No more packing. I'll worship at the altar of Celebrex for a week or two after we move, and then that's it.

Stay in touch, please. We really miss you, especially when we remember those of you who helped us pack and move the last couple of times. 'Wish you were here.

Peace and Love,
Leslie and Hope

April 23, 2006

Dear Friends,

I never knew so many dogwoods could grow in such a small area. They're everywhere! This was the week they decided to show their flowers, and we are awash in pink and white blossoms. Even though the last frost date here isn't until May, you'd never know it from looking at the landscape. I think I spotted some dogwoods on our property, but I couldn't climb over the construction equipment to get a good look.

My mountain education continues. I noticed that my tires are wearing very quickly. I have only 15,000 miles on the car and the tires look like they've traveled twice that. When I called it to the attention of the Honda dealer where I bought the car, the service manager assured me I'd be OK with those tires until my next oil change in 3,000 miles. I thought he was kidding, but he wasn't. It seems these curvy mountain roads are not kind to tires. Last week I learned that I'm supposed to over inflate my tires to prolong their lives on these roads.

This is the last week that Sweet Aromas will be open at its present location and we're not sure the grant it needs to relocate will come through. We went for one last dinner there. I was tempted to put several dozen cinnamon buns in the freezer but then I realized I'd have to move them to the new house, and nixed that idea. Occasionally I do let common sense prevail.

We're making good progress moving things. So far, we're still both able to walk, more or less, and gas hasn't gone over $3 a gallon yet. The moving goddess is working her magic because nearly every time I load up the car with things I can't carry very well, someone is at the house to lend a hand with the unloading part.

If anyone knows the trick to adjusting motion sensor lights, please clue us in. They're driving us crazy. I overheard Hope telling someone at a dinner party the other night that she wants to learn how to use a shotgun, and I strongly suspect that she's thinking of using one to "fix" those lights. If I thought there was even a slight chance she wouldn't blow a hole in the side of the house I might encourage her new interest in marksmanship.

Some of you are aware of The Two Stooges Construction Company, a name we gave ourselves years ago because of our general ineptitude when it comes to building or repairing anything. You'll be happy to know that we have officially gone out of business, as of this week.

After struggling to put together one of those infernal "easy-to-assemble" items, I took a hammer to one piece that wouldn't quite fit and reduced it to sawdust and splinters. There aren't enough cuss words in the world to contend with another one of those projects.

The company sent us a replacement part, and we finally managed to get the piece together, only to discover that two of the shelves were in backwards. Since I'd already screwed them halfway to China with our new motorized screwdriver, there was no way we were going to take it apart. So, now we have to wait for our friend Lyn to come with her tools, and hope she can help us make some modifications. If you come to our house, please refrain from commenting on the telephone stand that might not look quite right. It's a very sore point right now. We have sworn off putting together anything else...ever, and that means we are officially out of business.

We organized a publicity event for Sweet Aromas' move this week and as a thank you, Paula, the owner, wouldn't let us pay for our dinner the other night. We've both worked for chicken feed before; now we're moving up to chicken. Things are looking up.

We're looking at two more weeks before the big move into our house. There is still a lot to be done, but we are confident we'll be ready when the day arrives. Wish us luck.

Peace and Love,
Leslie and Hope

April 30, 2006

Dear Friends,

This has been one wild week. On Monday we pulled off the human chain to move Sweet Aromas' stuff to a storage location and got local media attention, which was the whole point to this unorthodox method of moving. I learned that doing publicity in the holler is a far cry from work I've done in other locations.

Folks here don't seem to understand the concept of publicity photo opportunities. They came out to get a job done. Rather than pass pots and pans hand-to-hand, as the news release I'd sent out said we would, they decided to load up their trucks with items and drive to the storage area. I guess that's part of the "git er done" mentality.

I compare trying to organize this thing to herding cats. Everyone had ideas about how best to do the moving, and they all conflicted with what I needed them to do to get the right photos for the newspaper. Luckily, the reporters didn't mind staged shots, so they got what they needed. Most important, Paula, the owner of Sweet Aromas, got what she needed, and the job did get done.

We had an interesting mix of volunteers ranging in age from about 30's to 70's, five of whom were from Happy Hollow. What really amazed me was that several of the volunteers turned down the brownies and cookies Paula provided as a reward. Now that's real altruism.

We were racing the clock to have our contractor do everything on the punch list so we could get someone to clean the house. Monday was to have been the day when the house resembled a beehive with subcontractors all working like mad to finish their part of the work. Our beloved electricians didn't show, and they had the lion's share of items to fix or complete. By this time, I could have used a recording that said, "Where are the _____ and why aren't they here?"

We gave up trying to put up our mailbox at Happy Hollow. After drilling with a screwdriver bit instead of a drill bit, and wondering why it didn't make holes, lots of cursing at the company that made the mailbox, and Hope threatening to leave me there alone, we finally decided we couldn't do it. I was resigned to taking a box at the local post office until our friend Lyn offered to do it for us. Who would have imagined it was so complicated to put up a mailbox?

I'm completely convinced there are good reasons why we are inept at these things. First, in my case, I was trained to call the super when something needed to be done. Second, since I was forced to take cooking and sewing instead of wood shop in school, I never learned to use tools. And the third reason is that the only tools I'd ever heard of until I was middle-aged, were hammers, screw drivers and pliers. No wonder we struggle with these projects.

As if we didn't have enough to do, this was the week I had to go for volunteer training for Merlefest, the gigantic music festival where I'll be working this weekend. My job is to make sure kids who want to use the rock climbing wall have harnesses on and limit the kids who want to go on the jumping thing to three minutes so they don't puke on us. I should be able to manage this. I work three hours on Saturday and Sunday and have the rest of the time to hear some of the best music around. My favorite banjo player, Bela Fleck, is performing and I've been dying to see him since I started taking lessons. I'm taking my binoculars to see if I can actually see his fingers on the strings. He plays so fast it looks like a blur.

'Gotta leave for the festival, so I'll close with the very happy thought that my next update will be from our new home, if we can get the computer connected. Have a great week.

Peace and Love,
Leslie and Hope

- 5 -

Home Sweet Home?

May 14, 2006

Dear Friends,

Whew! We have arrived in Paradise, and contrary to the promises they make to suicide Islamist terrorists, there are no virgins here. At least we haven't found any.

It's hard to know how to begin to tell you how it feels to be in our dreamed-of home at last. It's overwhelming to say the least. On the rare occasions, when we take a few minutes from the myriad chores that are demanded to make order out of chaos, it definitely feels like home.

Some of our new neighbors were kind enough to bring us supper on the night we moved in. We'd been moving from 7:30 a.m. until nearly 7 p.m. and that included two trips back and forth with the movers. Had these kind folks not brought us food, I know we'd have gone to bed hungry. We were too exhausted to cook, and didn't have much food in the house anyway. The only other nourishment we'd had all day was breakfast at McDonald's with the movers, because we wanted to be sure they kept their strength up.

Anyone who was within earshot has heard us proclaim loudly, "Never again." This is absolutely the last move I'll make on my feet.

I hate to borrow that slogan from Holocaust survivors and certainly don't mean to trivialize their experience, but our determination not to repeat this is that strong.

You would think we slept like the dead on our first night here, but in fact, neither of us got much quality sleep. Every time one of us moved, the pain from sore muscles was so great that we moaned and groaned and woke the other one up. If Homeland Security was eavesdropping on us, they probably thought we were having quite a wild night with all of that moaning, and they'd be right, but not the kind they imagined.

Hope was pushing against the clock before, during and immediately after the move. Her computer at work caught a virus, and we had disconnected the one at home for the move. It was tough, but she managed to get two grant proposals in on time. What I learned after the fact was that she completed them at 4 a.m. on a borrowed laptop on her bed at a conference. She had to leave just two days after our move, and was forced to work on them while her roommate slept.

When she called home to let me know where she was staying, she informed me that she'd left with no underwear or sleepwear, because she couldn't find them. That caught my attention, since I knew she was sharing a room with someone she supervised. She assured me the conference was at a mall and that she could shop for what she needed before nightfall.

On the home front, I did my best to put up towel bars, learn to use the new appliances and unpack boxes. At least half the time I spent searching for things I knew had to be in the house, but they were not where I was sure I put them. The combination of an aging body and a failing short-term memory is a cruel trick of nature. I ate lots of ginkgo biloba and Celebrex, and hoped for the best. Every time I succeeded in finding something I needed, I let out a victory yell, and hoped no one could hear me.

It's been an exhausting but exhilarating week, and the weather has cooperated by being lousy and removing any temptation to be outside. I've remained indoors trying to reduce the number of boxes, so that Hope would find the house better than she left it when she went to her conference.

We'll fill you in more next week. Until then, Happy Mother's Day to those of you who are biological or adoptive mothers, and also to the rest of you who I'm sure have been called "motha....." at least once in your lives. Enjoy the day.

Peace and Love,
Leslie and Hope

May 21, 2006

Dear Friends,

We're making progress but still aren't very organized. The highlights of our progress this week included getting a desk assembled, thanks to Nicole. She couldn't bear the thought of our tackling this, since it's much more complicated than our previous projects, so she did it with my assistance. I counted parts and handed them to her as she needed them. I much prefer this role to my usual one of chief assembler, swearer and caller to the company for assistance. We also got our sound system hooked up and are hoping to get the DVD player working before it becomes obsolete.

We've had a run of cloudy, rainy weather with even a hailstorm thrown in for good measure. If I were tempted to do any landscaping work, which I'm not, this would have provided a good excuse for not doing it. In the evenings it's been cool enough to use the fireplace, which has been nice. On Friday, the sun finally shone and we got a chance to appreciate all of the lovely weeds in front of the house.

We're happy to see that even with the trees donning their leafy summer wardrobe we still have a beautiful view of the mountains from the front and back of the house. I don't think I'll ever tire of looking at that view, and I make it a point to spend at least a few minutes each day just sitting and looking out the windows. For years I stared at the view in a photo on my desk at work and now that it's real, I'm just amazed by it all. We finally made it.

For those who are into masochism and might be wondering about my musical life, let me tell you that I have not even had time to take the banjo out of its case. I do know where it is, though. Our neighbors will just have to wait for their free entertainment. I might turn pro, if they elect to pay me not to play.

Entertainment this week was free and local; we have a washing machine that dances. Despite balancing the machine, it insists on dancing over to the dryer whenever we use the maximum extraction feature. We're convinced there's some past karma at work here; maybe they had an intimate relationship before they were reincarnated as washer and dryer. 'Anyone got any good ideas on how we can stop the dancing? And please don't tell us to get snakes, as some of you did when we asked about the mice problem.

If someone hadn't already used the title, *Diary of a Mad Housewife*, I'd surely have had the right to claim it this week. On Monday, the leak that we thought had been fixed in the expensive "guaranteed to be dry" basement still didn't appear to be fixed. The contractor ordered the plumbers to do whatever was necessary to fix it, so they tore out most of a bedroom wall next to the bathroom.

While this was going on downstairs, I decided to occupy my mind with other things, so I started baking a birthday cake for our friend Lyn. She and Dottie were invited over for a birthday celebration that night. Those of you who know me well are aware that I'm still a novice baker, so I chose a simple mix that required only an egg, oil and water. 'Simple, right? 'A foolproof recipe.

I discovered that olive oil doesn't count as vegetable oil and that's all I had, so I borrowed some from a neighbor, since I couldn't leave the plumbers alone here to go to the store.

I got everything mixed and into the oven and waited for the timer to go off so I could check for doneness. When I checked, I noticed it was still pretty liquid so I figured it was the mountain altitude, and gave it another ten minutes. 'Still liquid. After fooling with the controls on the oven, I realized it was not working. By this time, I figured it would be a store bought cake for Lyn if I could get out to buy one. I called the service number for the oven.

It took about half an hour to get a human, and I strongly suspect genetic testing would have ruled her out. Finally, I got the name and number of a local authorized service place. Either the woman at the repair place was hard of hearing, or she just couldn't understand my Yankee accent. After struggling through the conversation, she decided that yes, my oven was broken and said she'd have a tech come here on Friday

I figured I might have one more shot at getting this cake to bake, since it had baked part-way, and the broiler was still working. I put the broiler on high, figuring it would heat the oven enough to finish baking the cake. After ten minutes I saw smoke coming out of the oven door. This was not a good sign and I realized my idea would not work. I hoped I hadn't set the cake on fire, because the plumbers had turned off the water.

This was most definitely not my day. When a fierce thunderstorm developed late that afternoon I parked myself in my retirement chair right in front of the windows to tempt the fates. Since I wasn't struck by lightning, I figured the gods were through with me for that day.

By Thursday, I was feeling somewhat better since the leak had been fixed. We were assured that the wall would be repaired and repainted by Monday and the carpet would be replaced. Things were looking up for a few moments.

That is, until I realized the refrigerator was broken. Sears was unable to get someone out here until next Monday, I was told. We got a small portable refrigerator that had the power to freeze milk and eggs. 'Not what we wanted it to do, but it was better than nothing. The rest of our food went to a neighbor's freezer for safekeeping and the spoiled stuff went to the dump. I'm still not sure how we're going to feed my brother's family when they arrive for a three-day visit.

We are so looking forward to Monday when the refrigerator technician, the washing machine tech, the plumbers, the carpet restorers, and the graders will all be here. And of course, Nicole will be here in the role of ringmaster. I wish I had a video camera; this would be an Oscar-winning short subject piece, I'm sure.

I'm not leaving anything to chance. I'm off to find an exorcist for the appliances. 'Til next time.

Peace and Love,
Leslie and Hope

May 28, 2006

Dear Friends,

Living in the mountains is very different from our previous flat-land experience. We learn new things every day. For example, we discovered that the neighborhood songbirds are intent on using our windows to commit suicide. I came home one day to find a beautiful scarlet tanager dead on our front deck. I had not seen one before and had to look it up in my bird book for a positive identification. It's the first time I was able to observe all the identifying features. Maybe I should stick to post-mortem bird watching. It's much easier.

We've made a major step in the house-organizing process. We actually hung a couple of things on the walls and I definitely now have the knack of drilling into drywall and inserting screw anchors. Who says post-graduate education is useless?

We also finished assembling the last of the "easy to assemble" pieces with the help of friends. With our utility cabinet finished, we now have a place to put all of the tools we don't know how to use, including my favorite, the crow bar. What do you expect from someone from New Jersey? Old habits die hard.

Hope decided it was time to learn to use the oven, so we had some friends in for dinner the other night. These high-tech appliances are not at all intuitive. Despite our considerable education, it's impossible to use them without first reading the instruction manuals that come with them. The only thing we could use without first reading a book was the refrigerator. Everything else comes equipped with digital frustration.

Happy Hollow came alive this weekend with several of the part-time residents arriving from Florida to spend the summer months. There was a flurry of activity as people moved in and began an endless round of visits to each other's homes. On Saturday, as Hope got ready to make our daily trip to the dump with cardboard cartons, we got a call from Jan and June asking if they could visit. Hope gladly cancelled plans to go to the dump, leaving me with 50 pounds of cardboard in my car, where it will remain until Tuesday, since Monday is a holiday. That's the eleventh commandment in the holler. Thou shalt not dump trash on Sundays. It must be a Baptist thing.

We've been giving house tours to people who haven't been here yet, and are trying to decide which builder to hire to build their houses. It's been an unending stream of company, some staying for drinks and chat, and some just breezing through on their way somewhere else. It's sort of like the first day of camp, with everyone checking out friends' cabins.

We did finally get to enjoy one quiet, late dinner alone on our screened in porch. We just sat and listened to the night sounds. Birds headed for their roosts and crickets gave a last rub or two before turning in for the night. Many sounds we couldn't identify, but as long as they were outside and we were inside, we didn't care. It was just relaxing to be able to sit and enjoy the stillness of the night.

We're tired but happy in our new home and I'd say we've unpacked at least half of the cartons. Not bad for three weeks, but patience is not one of my virtues, so I won't be happy until everything is unpacked and put away. I've now reached the point where I can even find where the light and fan switches are in each room, but it will take a little longer until I figure out which is which. If it stays dark and I feel a breeze, I know I hit the wrong switch.

The only thing that would make this a perfect place is to move all of you here. We do miss you and hope you'll visit soon. Have a great week.

Peace and Love,
Leslie and Hope

June 4, 2006

Dear Friends,

I am happy to report that this was a much better week. At week's end we are cooking with gas, (literally) using a fixed refrigerator, and even washing clothes. Sounds like extreme fun, doesn't it? Believe me, it's a relief to be able to do all of that.

Watching the refrigerator repair guy at work was quite interesting. He already knew from the guy who was here to fix the washer that the problem with the refrigerator was a broken circulation fan, so one would expect that he'd have brought the part with him when he came on Monday.

Well, one should not assume things. After looking in his truck twice, he told me he was pretty sure the part was there, but that the truck was such a mess he couldn't find it. I offered to take everything out of his truck so he could find it, but he refused my generous offer. He called and placed an emergency order for the part, which meant he had to come back on Thursday to switch it with the modified part he put in on the first trip.

I'm getting pretty used to this sort of thing, and since the refrigerator is working I shouldn't have any more concern about it. There's just one thing nagging at me. This guy's wife is due any day now with their seventh child, and I find myself asking why it's really necessary to expand this weak gene pool. Oh well, if I look on the bright side, it will keep some teachers employed.

Hard as it must be for you to imagine such a thing, I'm sure you'll be as surprised as I to learn that the Two Stooge's Construction Company has been resurrected. Yes, Hope found a desk she likes in a catalog and it is lying here on the office floor, begging to be assembled. I'm really having trouble working up enthusiasm for it, but stepping over the box to get to my computer will probably bring me around soon.

You know how politically involved I've been most of my life. I was determined when we moved to North Carolina I would keep my distance from politics. I've managed to remain apolitical for one year but a story in the local paper jarred me back to activism.

The county commission voted to abolish a daycare center because they want to trim $150,000 from the budget for next year. I was outraged and fired off a letter to the commission and the local newspaper. This dimwitted decision will deprive eighty families of daycare or, as I've characterized it in my letter, the net result is eighty throwaway kids. For fewer than twenty-eight cents a day in taxes per taxpayer, they could raise more than is needed to keep the program. I'm just dying to have buttons printed that ask, "Whose kid isn't worth twenty-eight cents?" but I'll wait to see how the letters do before I escalate to the next level.

'Remember that story about the country mouse? Well, we know what happens to country mice; they climb into country cars. In some cases, as in my car, they just chew up tissues and leave their droppings all over the place. In others, like Hope's car, they get caught in the blower and start to decompose, causing quite a stink. It's amazing the trouble those little critters can cause. No wonder elephants hate them.

On Wednesday, our Vermont family arrived with so much baggage we thought they were moving in. Dinner the first night was a challenge because the oven broke again just as I was preparing vegetable lasagna. Luckily, our neighbors Dottie and Lyn came to the rescue and we ferried the lasagna back and forth to their oven. They were even kind enough to finish baking the brownies that had baked for ten minutes before the oven expired. Just use your imagination to figure out how my conversation went with Sears.

We used the family visit as an excuse to check out the small local zoo that is very low-budget but interesting. You might describe it as quaint; the reptile area is in the guy's basement. We managed to get through the zoo without my nephew Elijah saying anything about snakes and hillbillies, much to my relief.

The highlight of the visit for them surely had to be on Saturday when we all went kayaking and canoeing on the New River. Hope and I took a canoe and Barry and Elijah went in one kayak and sister-in-law Ann went in another. It was the most arduous canoeing I'd ever done because the water was low and we kept getting stuck on rock ledges. I thought I could execute a perfect maneuver around one ledge but Hope lost her nerve when she saw a boulder right in front of us and shifted her weight. The canoe capsized and I was just glad that we were both OK. I also hoped ten year-old Elijah hadn't heard any of the words that came out of his aunt's mouth; they were not for young ears.

They've left and we are now trying to recover. After three sixteen-hour days of running around I'm going to collapse in my retirement chair and take a nap.

Have a great week.

Peace and Love,
Leslie and Hope

June 18, 2006

Dear Friends,

The Two Stooges Construction Company had a brief revival. There was lots of shouting as is customary for revivals, but not too many "Amens." I guess the fact that we both lived through it is testimony to our having been "saved." We finished that desk for Hope and then she loudly declared that we are out of business, permanently, forever. 'No argument from me.

My other business, City Girl Landscaping, was moving ahead this week. With Hope away so much of the time I decided I had to step into the breach and do the planting before our soil all washes away. She's been the gardener in our family and I'd really prefer to let her keep that title, but I guess I've been inspired by seeing all the neighboring women out plowing and planting. I last about two hours before I have to collapse in the house and drink a gallon of water to revive.

Country life is the best. We're learning so much about wildlife here. On Monday as I was driving out of a parking lot in town, a guy stopped to tell me one of my tires looked low. Since I was near the Honda dealer I decided to have them check it out. Just as I was pulling into their lot, out of the corner of my eye, I saw something run across the floor in front of the passenger seat. I know of only one thing that moves that fast and hangs out in cars.

I felt like a complete idiot telling the service manager that I had two problems that needed attention in priority order. First, I told him I had a mouse in my car that needed to be removed by someone (not me) and second, I had a flat tire that needed to be repaired. As it turned out, the flat tire was a godsend because the mechanic discovered a mouse nest in the air conditioning system. In the course of removing it he did see the mouse, and said he hoped it had run out the open car doors. I was damned lucky the mouse didn't feast on any wires. They were working on another car that needed the entire electrical system replaced, thanks to a country mouse.

They sent me off with instructions to turn the heat to maximum and buy some mouse traps. I bought the only ones that Lowe's had left, the sticky kind, and placed them around the inside of the car. By the time I came out of the grocery store, one trap had a victim in it.

I looked around the parking lot, hoping to find a college student I could ask to remove it, but there wasn't anyone around. Usually there are lots of college kids around that parking lot, but that day it looked like a neutron bomb had hit Boone. I ruled out asking some ninety year-old woman using a walker, and decided I had to bite the bullet and do it. Echhh! I hoped the mouse was a loner.

Did you ever wonder what became of Laurel and Hardy? I learned during the past couple of weeks that they didn't die; they've gone into the appliance repair business. I've had ample opportunity to meet them individually when they were here working on the various possessed appliances that don't work right. Today Oliver Hardy (aka Butch) came to tackle the wall oven. When he finished installing the new computer board, it still didn't work. He's got a couple of theories he wants to explore when his partner, Stan Laurel, (aka Lyle) returns from vacation next week. We will be oven-less at least until next Tuesday, when the duo returns to take yet another crack at fixing this lemon.

Meanwhile, I think I'll start on the article I intend to distribute to all media outlets nationwide about the weird phenomenon that has occurred with our Jenn-Air oven. (made by Maytag) I think I'll lead with a paragraph that begins, "Thinking about buying a Jenn-Air oven? Make sure you have the name and phone number of the local exorcist handy." I think that might get the attention of the Maytag corporate PR people, don't you? I just might offer them the opportunity to provide me with a new oven before I decide to distribute my article free to all who want it.

On a lighter note, do you remember the lesbian cows that lived down the road from us? I have further proof of their sexual orientation. Today I walked into a grocery store and saw a sign on the door that read, "We have homo pet milk." I guess the girls are still at it.

I learned another new expression this week. I was chatting with the chiropractor as he was placing me on the rack for an adjustment and he told me he was "wide open." I asked if he thought it had to do with people being on vacation, assuming he meant he didn't have many patients. He said he was sure it was because his kids were out of school. At that point I was completely confused, but as I listened to him describe how busy he is running his kids all over to various activities, I suspected it meant he was really busy. I'm wondering if it has to do with some Nascar expression referring to a wide open throttle. I'll have to investigate before I try to use it.

I'm seeing a new doctor tomorrow and I hope he doesn't get the wrong idea about those bruises from the canoeing incident. It would not be funny if he sent the sheriff to arrest Hope.

We hope the livin' is easy for you during this beautiful summer.

Peace and Love,
Leslie and Hope

July 2, 2006

Dear Friends,

I had the most fun this week when Laurel and Hardy came to work on the oven. Three Band Aids, two towels and a roll of paper towels later, (They cut themselves.) they finally admitted defeat and signed the death certificate on this oven. A new one was ordered and is due later in the week.

On the appointed day, I called Sears to confirm that the midnight truck from Georgia had indeed arrived, and that my new oven was on it. I was in a heightened state of anxiety all day, wondering if the oven installers and the gas guy would get here at the same time. Getting all of this coordinated was at least as complicated as docking the shuttle with the space station, maybe more so. The suspense built throughout the day. Anything could derail this complex plan; great fishing weather was right at the top of the list.

The oven arrived and so did the gas guy. It took three people to get the oven in, and I'm happy to report that it worked. With friends arriving the same day the oven did, we were so relieved to be able to cook without ferrying things to and from a neighbor's kitchen. Small things can make us so happy.

I've been a bit preoccupied with appliances lately, as you can probably tell. I saw a hand-lettered sign on a pole the other day that read, "Do you want the keys to heaven?" and my mind immediately visualized a place where all appliances worked properly. I was tempted to call the phone number but then thought better of it. It could be that this was the holler equivalent of "For a good time, call....." that I used to see on bathroom walls in New Jersey.

Our friend Dottie had an interesting experience with one of the electricians who worked on both our houses. The guy walked into her house to do some work, and had a Pepsi bottle with about an inch of liquid in it. She asked him if she could freshen it up for him and he said, "Oh no, that's my spittoon, so's I don't splash tabacca juice all over yer house." I told her she should feel honored. The last time I spoke to him we were stopped on the road, and he was using a Styrofoam cup as a spittoon. I guess only house calls warrant his finest glassware.

Wisdom can be found in all sorts of places, I've learned. I wouldn't normally turn to the guy who cuts my hair for advice on food but I happened to ask him what local folks like on their hot dogs. This was in preparation for volunteering to staff a hot dog stand at a festival to raise money for a local homeless shelter. This straightforward question prompted an entire lecture about what to eat and not to eat. He assured me the local folks don't put sauerkraut or anything "fancy" like that on their dogs, just chili, onions and slaw, with mustard or mayonnaise.

Included in the lecture was this bit of advice as well. He told me never to eat anything that hogs won't eat. Since I haven't spent much time around hogs, I asked him to elaborate. Two items in particular are on the "do not eat" list for hogs—cucumbers and cantaloupes. He told me if you throw those things into the hog's bucket, it will look at you like you're crazy. He didn't seem to know why, but he is sure that both of those foods are bad for you. Another group of foods to avoid are those that grow at night, he told me. I'm guessing he's referring to the nightshades.

While I was getting my hair cut, a guy came past as he was leaving the shop and told my stylist to give me a big stick when I was done. He said I'd need it to beat the men off so I could safely get in my car to go home. I took that as a compliment, and tried to blush. After the guy was out of earshot, my stylist told me the guy was a pack of trouble and he had never worked a day in his life. He said even his farm animals were strange, pygmy goats and other weird animals. I think he was trying to warn me that I should not take up with this guy when I left the shop. Fat chance of that!

For me, this was a much more relaxing week. I actually did sit on the porch and play my banjo a couple of times. We're rounding out the week this afternoon by seeing our local community theater group perform *Man of La Mancha*. We can really identify with "The Impossible Dream." For us, it's having fully functioning appliances.

Think of us whenever you turn on your appliances. Have a great week.

Peace and Love,
Leslie and Hope

July 9, 2006

Dear Friends,

I know you're dying to know how the oven is performing. It actually still works, but the fan was noisy. That's past tense. On Wednesday, my new best friend Lyle arrived to work on the leaking washer (yes, you read right) and while he was here he took a look at the oven to see what the loud noise was. He said it was the motor, not the fan, so he ordered a new one. It's gotten to the point, when Lyle comes to the house he and I just look at one another and shake our heads. He doesn't ask how I am any more because I think he's afraid to hear the answer.

One of our neighbors suggested that our house might be built on some sort of magnetic lode and that's making all the appliances malfunction. She was kidding, but I'm really starting to wonder about it. The new generator isn't working either; the electrician has to bring the guy from the generator company to fix it.

The other night I was driving into the dirt road leading to our development, when I saw a guy with a shotgun standing by the side of the road with a woman. I stopped and asked what they were looking for. "Varmints," was the answer. I asked, "Small ones or big ones?" He laughed and said they were looking for some varmints that were small and weasel-like. I didn't stay around to see if he found them, but I made a mental note not to piss off that guy. That shotgun looked pretty serious.

On Thursday I experienced one of those mental Kodak moments at the Wal-Mart. I was in line to pay for my purchases and there were two young guys in front of me. They were either high school or college kids, and had a large box of condoms on the conveyor belt. The cashier was a very young man, maybe eighteen, but he looked twelve. The more brazen of the two cool dudes in line asked the cashier, "Is it OK to use Vaseline with these? It's a first date and everything."

All sorts of comments were running through my brain, and I was dying to chime in with advice about Vaseline weakening condoms, but I chose to listen to the little voice in my head that said, "Keep your mouth shut; it's not your business." The cashier told them it was fine to do that, and still I maintained my silence.

The cashier was clearly embarrassed by the whole incident and apologized to me when he started to ring up my things. I felt so sorry for him. When I took my bags he told me to have a "blessed day." Funny, he didn't tell them that. I figured he'd take the first chance he got to pull out his Bible and have a quick chat with Jesus about the incident with the Trojans.

We have grading work being done at the house and the other day I noticed one of my newly planted hollies had been replaced by tread marks from an earth mover. When I was talking to the workers about replacing it, one of them said he'd seen mice playing around my car. I told him we'd been having a hard time keeping them out of the cars and he said the really bad thing about mice is that they attract snakes. He told me not to be surprised if I find a snake coiled up around the engine. I wonder if Volkswagen still makes airtight cars. I might have to look for one.

We love living in the country, but there are some things it will take awhile to get used to. One little inconvenience is that a bear has been sighted in Happy Hollow. Some of our neighbors who have never seen one think that's just so neat, and they can't wait to see one. Others of us who have had close encounters with bears are not so thrilled about this news.

I'm having trouble remembering my name this week after being called "honey, sweetie or babe" by the workers. I was about to burst, but not wanting to anger people who were using earth movers right next to the new house I just started calling them by the same names. They never noticed. I reminded myself that I never slugged a waitress in Baltimore for calling me "Hon," so I could put up with this for another few days.

One of the workers asked me what I did and I told him I was retired. He said, "No, I mean what kind of work did you do before." I told him I was in public relations and I could see he didn't know what that was, so I explained that I helped get people's names in the news. "Oh," he said, "around here that ain't hard at all. All's ya gotta do is jes shoot someone and yer name'll be in the paper fer sure." I explained that the people I worked for wanted good publicity, and that it's a little harder to get that stuff in the paper. Actually, there were times when I probably should have given that advice to a client. Come to think of it, I should just have shot some of them myself.

For the last few weeks I've felt like a pimp, because I've been trying to find a male pollinator for my Winter Berry Holly. I visited several nurseries to find her a mate, but found none. Finally, after weeks of searching, I lucked out. I was sure, given the pay differential for men and women, that he'd cost more, but was pleasantly surprised to learn he was half as expensive as she was. I hope they live happily ever after so I can give up the procurement thing.

On that note I'll wish you happy hunting.

> Peace and Love,
> Leslie and Hope

August 1, 2006

Dear Friends,

Wow! Is it really August? It's hard to believe we'll soon be seeing fall foliage. We've had lots of rain lately and I'm grateful for every wet day, because I don't have to water the plants.

I don't expect to see our pictures in the post office yet, but I'm sorry to say that we have become outlaws in North Carolina. Hope got stopped the other day and cited for having expired tags. I checked the registration for both cars when she got home and sure enough, they're expired. When I went online to renew them, we learned that the motor vehicle administration here doesn't always send out renewal notices. It takes seven days for the new registrations to get to us, and we're hoping neither of us gets stopped by a trooper before they arrive.

Since we've embarked on a life of crime, we figured we'd embrace the new role with gusto. We've been going out at night stealing rocks. Yes, I know I should be ashamed to admit it, but we've come to this sorry state of affairs. There's a perfectly good explanation for our behavior, though, and it all began with a well-meaning act by my family.

While my brother's family was here last month, they began building a rock wall around our front garden. This was a great idea because it kept them busy for awhile. Unfortunately, they ran out of rocks. I know that sounds ridiculous, since we live in the woods, but rocks are at a premium here for walls and drainage ditches. We could go out and buy a ton of rocks; they don't cost very much. The problem is getting them back here. We can't put that much weight in our cars without wrecking the suspension systems, and we don't have a truck. I suspect this might fuel Hope's argument in favor of buying one, but I'm not budging. So, we go out under cover of night and steal rocks from places where they're not likely to be missed. You'll understand if I don't get more specific, I'm sure. I want all of you to have deniability, should you be questioned.

When I'm not out stealing rocks, I've embarked on a new mission, having observed that the "fixed" washer has resumed dancing

148

again. I'm now dealing with the special assistant to the president of Maytag Corp. If the wall in our laundry room hadn't stopped the dancing washer the other day, there's no telling where it would have stopped. I contacted the senior vice president for corporate communications for Maytag and sent him the opening paragraphs of an article I've written and plan to distribute free to all who want it. It goes like this.

"Do you like to dance but fear that no one will ask you at the local dance hall? Here's the perfect solution. Buy a Maytag Neptune washer and you'll never lack for a dance partner again. The Maytag Neptune model is the one on the fifteen-inch pedestal, touted as the one that won't break your back when you wash clothes. It turns out it has other talents as well; it dances.

That's right. It whirls and spins and actually moves across the floor as it washes. For a really fast number, just set the spin to the maximum extraction setting and watch it go! Of course, it helps if you don't have anything in its path, like a dryer or a wall. This baby really moves!"

I told him I'd offer to open my home to the TV stations if they wanted to get videotape of the dancing washing machine in action. Look for my washer on the evening news soon. As you might expect, I got an immediate response and have been assigned to the woman in the president's office. She did acknowledge I'm not the first to observe this phenomenon. What a surprise! She said the Maytag engineers do have parts to fix the problem and called me back twice to assure me she's working on it. I guess she doesn't want to see my washer on TV.

Just in case she needs extra motivation, I penned another article about "What Really Happened to the Lonely Maytag Repairman" and explained that he dropped dead of exhaustion from dancing with one of their washers in a dance marathon. I sent it to her. I must confess that I'm enjoying aggravating Maytag. It's their turn.

Take care and let us hear from you.

Peace and Love,
Leslie and Hope

August 8, 2006

Dear Friends,

I was fully prepared to send a brief email saying there would be no update this week but upon reflection, I realized we need the support of our friends, and decided to do one anyway.

After telling me she was prepared to open a new job search, Hope's organization beat her to the punch. As she is telling people here, she "done went and got farred." And you thought things move slowly in the holler! Last month her boss told her she was doing a terrific job and this month they let her go. Of course we are both upset about this, but I see immense relief on her face too. She never got the kind of support she needed to be successful on that job, and it seems that several people there just don't like working with outsiders, especially ones who are more highly educated than they are.

The events of this last week sound more like a rerun of a Lucy show than reality. I was baking a meat loaf (turkey) and heard the kind of sound that signals the oven has shut off. It was fifteen minutes early so I went to check. To my disgust, the same problem we had with the original oven was occurring with this one. I'm sure there's a term for premature shutdown that's less obscene than what I'm calling it, but that's what's wrong with this second oven.

When I called the store where we bought it, the owner told me that the first one that they took out of here was "working just fine." "What do you mean, it's working fine?" I asked him. "Well," he told me, "I sold it to someone else (at a discount, he hastened to add) and I haven't heard a word from them. It was for a new house." I told him the poor suckers who will be moving into the house probably haven't tried it yet. Talk about a lack of ethics. If you're shopping for appliances, take heed.

Anyway, I made an appointment for a technician to come look at the oven...again. As soon as I hung up the phone, Hope called with her bad news about the job. I hopped in the car to go to her office to help her clean it out and make sure she got home OK. While I was driving there, a bee flew in the car and stung me. At this point I began to feel a little paranoid, but nothing else went wrong that day, and things have improved since.

We have weathered adversity before and know we will get through this difficult time too. Fortunately, we have several things going for us:

- We both like peanut butter and jelly
- We both need to lose weight
- We have a nice roof over our heads
- I still remember how to make campfire stew from my camp counselor days
- We're maintaining a sense of humor
- For entertainment we have only to go to the local supermarket or our laundry room
- We're in good health
- We have good friends who offer moral support and free meals

I'm awaiting a call back from the Maytag repair person telling me when he's coming to install the stabilizing part in the washer, and also to look at the oven. Wouldn't you know? Maytag makes Jenn-Air ovens too!

Meanwhile, it's been hot enough here that I really don't want to use the oven anyway. We've actually slept with the ceiling fan on for two nights this week. We can't complain about the heat here in the mountains when we see what the rest of you are putting up with around the nation.

Try to keep cool and we'll do likewise.

Peace and Love,
Leslie and Hope

August 27, 2006

Dear Friends,

Well, the saga of the appliances continues. The Maytag guy came and fixed the washer as much as it can be fixed. He told me these models were never designed for home use and pointed out that they bolt them to the floor in laundromats. I always thought that was to prevent theft, not runaways.

The oven remained broken because they sent the wrong part with him. He comes back in a few days and we'll know then whether the oven will work or not. I'm already preparing the nice woman from Maytag's corporate offices for the next steps, should the oven not work after this next repair. Let's just say it's a good thing I kept a couple of business suits in the closet.

Awhile back, I reported that the status of "southern lady" had been conferred upon me by the local gas station that provides full service for ladies and some elderly gentlemen. Well, the rising gas prices have caused them to cut back on this courtesy. See, even southern chivalry has its price. The guy handed me a flyer with apologies when I went in for a fill-up this week, and said they have to limit the full-serve hours to keep their prices competitive. I guess that makes me a part-time southern lady. Easy come, easy go.

The representative from Maytag called to find out how the washer is doing. I give them credit for trying to fix their appliances. In fact, I might offer to do a commercial for them. I've got one in mind. See how you like it.

The scene opens to find a harried and disheveled homemaker (me) in the midst of obviously broken appliances. The room should look like some sort of explosion has just occurred. The homemaker, showing signs of being there during the explosion, steps out of the mess and says into the camera, "Their appliances may stink, but you can always count on Maytag to come and try to fix them." Fade to black. What do you think?

I did tell my Maytag friend we should all pray (it's a holler thing) that the oven gets fixed, because if not, we'll have to have all the kitchen cabinets redone to accommodate a new model. The repair guy was here the other day and we waited anxiously to see if it could beat its old record of three weeks without a breakdown. Anyone want to place any bets?

Hope was in Michigan for a week to visit her family and that left me in charge of gardening. I planted grass seed but was too impatient to wait for it to germinate. It seems to me three days are plenty, but so far there is no grass in sight.

Hope got back the other day and brought a surprise; she's now a redhead. Not Lucy Ricardo red, but quite different. Her sisters gave her a makeover for a birthday present. We used to have discussions about hair coloring when Hope urged me to let mine grow out gray. When I finally did it, she thought that was just dandy. Now, however, that she's getting gray, she doesn't think it's such a fine idea.

Speaking of aging, we had a double birthday party here for Hope and our friend Susan. We hosted several of our neighbors for cake and ice cream. I had intended to bake the cake myself but you can guess what happened while I was attempting to do that. Still, we all enjoyed celebrating the two birthdays.

We had a visit this week from our dear friends Kathryn and Karen. It's taken a long time for them to coordinate schedules to come see us but it was worth the wait. We did a house blessing and sure hope the appliances were paying attention. As of this writing the oven is working again but we really don't expect it to last.

That's it from the holler for this week. Stay in touch.

Peace and Love,
Leslie and Hope

September 3, 2006

Dear Friends,

Our new neighbors here at Happy Hollow are really great. As soon as word spreads about someone's need, everyone does what they can to help them out. For example, one of our neighbors called the other night and asked me, "Does anyone in your house do snakes?" I thought she might be referring to the practice of snake handling that's done in some of the rural churches here, so I was cautious. It turns out she was asking if one of us would come to her house and get a snake out of the closet.

After getting some information about the size and color of the snake, I consulted with Hope and told our neighbor we'd be right there. We grabbed a canvas bag, the grabber tool, gloves and a broom, and off we went to the rescue.

When we got to their house, one of them was frozen in a state of panic in front of the closet door, and the other was pacing frantically on the front porch. One look at the two of them told us we needed to get them out of there quickly before we ended up with a medical emergency. The catatonic one was persuaded to leave the closet door and she took refuge in her shower stall. We worried that she might pass out, and urged her to go on the front porch with her partner. Finally she agreed.

Then we set about trying to find the snake. We knew we were looking for a thin black snake, less than a foot long. After removing every article of clothing from the closet, checking in every pocket, shoe and boot, we didn't find the snake. When I asked them exactly where they had seen the snake, we solved the problem. I picked up a pair of sweat pants with a black drawstring and took it out to them and asked if this looked like the snake they saw. Sure enough, the snake turned out to be a drawstring that was hanging on the floor of the closet. The one that had seen the snake had not put her glasses on, and when I asked why, she had a perfectly logical answer. She didn't want to see it.

I only regret that I didn't have a video camera for this snake-chasing adventure. It would have made a good short subject.

Our days are already growing shorter here and often the mornings are misty or foggy. I still haven't learned to distinguish between the two conditions. I have noticed that when we are enshrouded in fog, sounds seem to be distorted.

One morning this week I awakened to see fog covering nearly everything and I thought I heard a fog horn in the distance. At first I didn't think much about it, until it registered in my brain that we are six- or seven-hours from the coast, and there'd be no reason for a fog horn to be here. I'd grown so used to the sound of fog horns out in the Chesapeake Bay when I worked in Annapolis, that it just seemed so natural. The source of this sound however, turned out to be a cow in a nearby pasture.

Now that Hope is once again covered by health insurance (no job yet, just big check-writing) we thought she could afford to take a risk or two. We went out rock hunting the other day and found an abandoned worksite that had great rocks, nice big ones. We pulled off the road and started loading rocks into the car. The ground was very muddy from three days of rain and I lost my footing while carrying a big rock. That's when the fun started.

Hope was crouched down examining rocks next to me and I knew I had to avoid dropping this huge rock on her, so I twisted and tossed the rock to the ground. In so doing, I completely lost my balance and fell on top of her, knocking her into the mud. We both managed to get up and she told me in no uncertain terms that we were finished gathering rocks. In fact, as I recall her words, laced with expletives, she said, "That's it! No more *&^%$# rocks. We're going home." I know when not to argue, so home we went to get the mud off her. I was completely clean since I fell on Hope, but she was covered with mud. We've been laughing ever since about our "mud wrestling" episode.

Fall's a comin' to the holler. If I'm out early in the morning I catch the faint smell of wood smoke. Another hint is that the clothes on the neighboring farmhouse clotheslines are changing from short sleeve shirts to long Johns, a sure sign of the changing seasons.

I'm out photographing wildflowers so I can look at them during the winter. It's a good thing I still have Maytag to aggravate me or I might slip into a total state of relaxation. The other night while

Hope was baking a pie, the oven died again. Look for me on the cover of the Inquirer! I'll be the one featured in the story that begins, "An otherwise sane and rational woman snapped and, wielding a bazooka and a flamethrower, took hostages in the Maytag corporate offices."

We'll be joining the bears and other hibernating creatures soon. Enjoy the last days of fall and plan to visit us after the thaw.

Peace and Love,
Leslie and Hope

EPILOGUE

As we went to print, Leslie and Hope were enjoying life in a house full of functioning appliances. Hope is working at yet another new job, happy to have landed a permanent position so she can keep Leslie in the style to which she hoped to become accustomed in her retirement.

Life in their holler community is good, with strong kinship ties developing among their neighbors and friends. They continue to learn about the ways of the mountain people and they appreciate their open friendliness.

They crossed a major threshold recently when one of their long-time holler neighbors invited them into her farmhouse for a cup of tea. Reminded constantly that they remain foreigners in Appalachia, they regarded this as a hopeful sign that one day they might actually fit in, something they are trying hard to do.

These two women are among many new residents of Appalachia and are making every effort to avoid some of the behaviors that have made the native residents wary of strangers from other parts of the country. To some of their new neighbors they know they are objects of amusement and puzzlement. Likewise, Leslie and Hope still find some of the local customs difficult to understand. They continue to find humor in their efforts to adjust to their new environment.

They believe that living in beautiful Appalachia is well worth the effort it takes to overcome their status as foreigners. The physical surroundings encourage a type of serenity that nourishes the soul, and makes the possibility of ever returning to an urban lifestyle highly unlikely. As Leslie has said on numerous occasions, "I intend to leave here feet first when the time comes. I'm not moving ever again."

About the Author

Leslie Brunetsky is a retired, award-winning public relations and marketing executive who has served as a political consultant to gubernatorial and legislative campaigns. She's been a columnist and has ghost-written numerous articles for public and business officials over the span of her career.

A former teacher, she regards the years spent teaching middle and high school students among the most satisfying and rewarding of her working life.

Now retired, she has turned her city-trained eyes on the nuances of mountain culture in the southern Appalachians where she and her life partner live. Real Country is her first book.

Printed in the United States
142867LV00009B/43/P